A Long Walk with Sally

A Long Walk with Sally

DAVID CLARK, JR.

Red Sunset Publishing

Library of Congress Control Number: 2015955811
Clark, Jr., David, Author
A Long Walk With Sally:
A Grieving Father's Golf Journey Back to Life
David Clark, Jr.

ISBN: 978-0-692-52120-5

AUTOBIOGRAPHY / Personal Memoirs

Cover photo taken by George Karbus on Lahinch Golf Club.

QUANTITY PURCHASES: Schools, companies, professional groups, clubs, and other organizations may qualify for special terms when ordering quantities of this title. For information, email davidcjr@mac.com.

All rights reserved by David Clark, Jr. and Red Sunset Publishing
This book is printed in the United States of America

Red Sunset Publishing

Sally and Grace – A Friendship of a Lifetime

Dedication

~

This book is dedicated to the beautiful memory of my sweet daughter, Sally McKenzie Clark; my beloved niece, Anna Grace Jordan; and to my friend, Randy Dorton, a friend's friend. They were taken from us too soon, but in the time they were here they made a positive difference in this world. Their tremendous legacies of putting others above themselves continue to live on.

While you are now in the loving hands of our Creator and his Son, Jesus Christ, we miss and love you and look forward to the day we see you again.

Above all, this book is for Jo, Reynolds, Graham, Jennifer, and my sunshine, McKenzie. Without you, my life would be meaningless. I love you.

Foreword

Ron Green, Jr.
Senior Writer, *Global Golf Post*

When I met David Clark for the first time, he was sitting on the veranda at Quail Hollow Club where he'd sat so many days after his daughter, Sally, and her cousin, Grace Jordan, had been killed in an auto accident. It had been several years since the accident but his pain was still fresh and painted on his face.

David thought he might have a story to tell but he wasn't sure. If he was to ever find a sense of peace and salvation in the aftermath of the accident, he believed he'd find it on the golf courses in the British Isles. As he explained the journey he'd begun, hoping to play nearly 300 courses across five countries, David understood his unique approach to dealing with his grief.

Walking golf courses an ocean away wouldn't make sense to many people, but if you've been touched by the game the way some of us have, it can have a profoundly therapeutic quality. That's what David was seeking and, in a large measure, that's what he found over the course of playing 290 courses scattered across England, Scotland, Ireland, Northern Ireland, and Wales.

His story is actually two stories. It's about a broken man trying to come to terms with losing his 19-year-old daughter. It's also about a man in love with the windswept charm of links golf, where the sea, the sand, and the sky frame courses that seemed laid there when the world was born, waiting only to be discovered.

David Clark's golf journey is remarkable. His personal journey is more remarkable. He has gone to the darkest place a parent can go and he's walked some of the most beautiful places in the world. He's come out on the other side with the sense of peace he sought and a story that's both heartbreaking and inspiring.

With his wife, Jo, and others, David created Sally's Y to honor the legacy of his daughter, building a place where others can shine.

Sally would be touched by what her father has done.

Machpelah

A Special Note Regarding Golf Course Classification and the Courses I Chose to Play

~

In the back of this book, you will find a list of the courses I have played in the British Isles, along with my classification for each course. I also reference these courses within my narrative. I think it is important to establish that I do not in any way consider myself an authoritative source on classifying golf courses across the British Isles. While traveling there for 30 years now, I do have an enlightened understanding of the differences, but my knowledge has been gained by what others with far more expertise shared in books, especially books by authors Donald Steel, George Peper and Malcolm Campbell, and Tom Doak. I took all of this information and attempted to categorize the different courses in the British Isles by what I found when I played them. These are not meant to be literal standards for broad application. They are only my version, and I acknowledge some fluidity in my classifications.

Courses there are typically classified by the type of vegetation, turf, and soil, and location of the course. Most courses fall under the categories of parkland, heathland, moorland, meadowland, clifftop, seaside, and links. U.S. courses typically equate to parkland-type courses. They are for the most part well-conditioned courses located among trees with fine turf and most often found away from the coast.

Heathland courses are typically inland as well. They are characterized by open, low-growing vegetation, such as heather and gorse, with well-draining, infertile, acidic soil. The region where Gleneagles is situated, near the middle of Scotland, is a great example.

Moorland is the higher elevation of heathland. Courses built over this type of land play similar to links courses. However, I think the current condition of the courses at Gleneagles has trended more toward parkland style golf than what I first played in 1986. This is not a criticism but an observation. Meadowland is open land most often void of trees, with rich, fertile soil typical of farmland.

With respect to the final three categories, defining these gets tricky and requires a dose of subjectivity. Beauty is in the eyes of the beholder, so to speak. I must again emphasize that I do not consider myself an expert on these descriptions. It is simply what I have come to believe over many years of traveling there. In my opinion there are clear, indisputable examples of each, but some fall into a gray area of a combination of elements of each category.

They are all immediately by one of the many bodies of saltwater surrounding the British Isles, and this is a crucial feature to the golf you play over them. For the most part, clifftop courses are situated along the cliffs around the British Isles. There is significant elevation change from the coast to where the course is routed. They rarely have the same soil you find at sea level. However, given their exposure to the sea and the weather you find there, they play in many ways similar to a links course. Seaside courses are courses also located along the coast but lack some clear feature typical of a clifftop or links courses. I know some will take exception to this, and I don't mean this as a criticism, but I feel courses recently built, such as Kingsbarn and Castle Stuart—which are two of my favorites—are seaside courses. Neither is a true links or clifftop course. While the land they were built over was located by the North Sea and the Moray Firth, respectively, it was farmland that was mass graded with a significant amount of non-native soil brought in to create a links-type course. However, they play exactly like a links course and deserve all the accolades they've received.

With respect to a true links, let me explain what I believe is the origin of the word "links" and how it came to be associated with golf. Whether my version is right or wrong, there is no doubt the word is chronically misused.

The word "links," prior to golf's origin, was used primarily to describe the area of land near sea level situated between the shoreline and the beginning of rich farmland. The land was considered unsuitable for farming due to its sandy soil, typically populated with massive dunes, harsh seaside weather, and frequent flooding from coastal storms. It thus served to *link* the coast to the farmland, earning the description of links land.

I know there is still debate about the absolute origin of golf; few though will argue that the game we know today had its beginnings in St. Andrews, Scotland, during the 15th century. The land where what we consider "golf" began fits the description of links land perfectly. I believe that as the game took hold, the early golfers came to associate the game with the land on which they were playing. It's easy to imagine a Scot centuries ago saying, "So and so is out playing some frivolous game on the links land." That's how the term "links" came to be associated with golf, or at least that's my personal understanding and long-held belief.

While there are courses that are indeed links around the British Isles and a few other areas of the world, I believe there is even a higher classification of true links. These, in my opinion, were laid out by God, and it has been our job to discover them. There is little about them that was manufactured. Our charge was to find His routing, create a teeing area to start a hole, and then a place to situate a green to finish the hole—without disturbing much of His work. I will do my best to note the ones I believe best fit the true links description. Again, this is just my view based on what I have learned from others and the 30 years of traveling there. I love the game of golf as it is played in the British Isles, over a special area of God's Creation.

The British Isles

Please God …

⁓

I considered hitting an iron off the tee to assure I kept my ball in play, but my caddie handed me my driver before I had a chance to ask for it. *Please God*, I asked silently, *don't let me lose this ball now.* I was in a fragile emotional place, and losing the ball, which symbolized so much now after being with me consistently through multiple courses, would be devastating. There was little doubt that Sally was here, and losing this ball on the last hole would crush me. It would be like losing her a second time.

Just as I feared, I pulled my tee shot. I watched in horror as my ball headed directly toward some of the deepest, thickest rough on the hole, or even worse, across the road to the left of the fairway. Everything I was beginning to understand about this trip and *Sally's ball* might all be going away right here with this one fateful swing. As I watched, it fell just short of the road and dove into the thick rough. I wanted to run immediately after it as my eyes locked on where I thought it had landed, but Jo, Jennifer, and Greg hadn't hit their tee shots yet. As had happened many times previously during this trip, when I became aware of the significance this ball had to me, I went into a total panic.

Once everyone had hit, I almost sprinted toward where I thought I would find it. I felt frantic. The ball wasn't where I expected it might be, and a sense of despair began to hit me like a wave blindsiding me. *What if I've lost Sally's ball on my last hole?*

Then I saw a ball barely visible in the tangle of grass. It was mine. I'd be able to recognize that ball no matter where it landed! Yes, it was mine—no longer with the markings I'd originally written on it when we first set out, but still completely recognizable to me. I'll never forget the range of emotions that rushed through me. It didn't matter that it was unplayable. I had found it. That's all I cared about.

I picked it up and clutched it in my hand as I processed what it meant to me. Again, as on the tee for the first time since the accident, as I held and looked at that ball, I could sense tears welling up in my eyes. I knew I couldn't allow myself to cry at that moment and I willed myself to calm down before dropping it where I could hit a short iron into the fairway. From there I hit a series of short shots to make sure I kept the ball where I could see it. On the green, I casually putted out, but again, barely winning a wrestling match with my emotions. I pulled the ball out of the hole for the final time and tucked it into my pocket. I knew I would never play another hole with it.

We put our clubs in the car and headed to the club's bar for a celebratory pint before driving back to Dromoland Castle where we were staying. Jo hardly looked at me. She spoke to me only if she had to. I hadn't told her the whole story about the ball I'd been playing, and the tension between us was impossible for Jennifer and Greg to ignore.

Back at Dromoland Castle, Jo said she was tired and would not be down for dinner. In the room, I told her I needed to explain what had happened. She said she was going to bed but was willing to listen. I described how my ball had become Sally's ball and how I'd been given the gift to play that one ball on every course during our trip. Although it seemed as if I was being inconsiderate of her and our friends, I had been determined not to lose Sally's ball at our final course on this trip. "You might not understand," I added, "but I felt Sally was there."

I reminded Jo of how Palmer Trice had explained that we would grieve together and we would grieve apart. Marking the ball the way I had allowed me to feel a connection to Sally and was one way I could deal with my grief. I expressed to Jo how much I loved her and how sorry I was for leaving her on her own at Lahinch, but I hoped she could forgive me and understand what I was telling her. She said it helped to hear my explanation and she asked me to leave her alone so she could process what I'd revealed. When I returned to our room awhile later, I found Jo asleep. I didn't know when or how I'd tell her, but I was certain that this part of the world was where I'd have to come to find whatever peace I could after losing our sweet Sally.

Introduction

~~

In today's world, parents don't expect to lose a child during their lifetime. With the exception of a tragedy or through the ultimate sacrifice to defend our freedom, we have fortunately been insulated from what was a common heartbreak just a few generations ago. When it does happen today, however, no matter the reason, a parent's heartbreak is the worst imaginable. The only thing worse than losing a child is losing more than one.

As any parent who has lost a child would agree, I would have willingly given my own life for Sally's rather than live with the heartbreak I have felt since that fateful night in April 2004. But God didn't want me yet. He needed Sally and Grace, and later, Randy. They had each made a tremendous difference in His Creation and earned their reward to live in eternity in His Home. He apparently still has things left for me to do here before I can hope to hear Him say, "A job well done, my child."

Prior to the accident, for 20 years I traveled to the British Isles to play golf and spend time there. On several occasions, I also took my entire family, including Sally, for a family vacation.

Beyond sightseeing, where we stayed had an abundance of lochs and streams in which the children could fish and play. We also attended Open Championships while there. It was a place I never tired of visiting. I always felt a peace there, and I dearly loved the links golf I played. Each time I returned to play golf, I tried to add at least one new course to my itinerary and used a book—*Classic Links of England, Scotland, Wales, and Ireland*—I'd purchased in St. Andrews in 1995, written by well-known British golf course architect, Donald Steel, as a guide. Mr. Steel is also an accomplished golfer and he, like I, especially loved links golf.

As I struggled with losing Sally, I desperately looked for a place I could grieve on my own and be left to find whatever peace God would grant me. Based on certain events that occurred, God revealed to me that there was no better place than the British Isles to look for it. This was the basis of my decision to go there and play so many courses. It was never about doing something unique or checking off a list no one else had checked off. I did it for my own salvation. It became my sanctuary, my safe harbor, where I could grieve alone, an ocean away from the people who knew me. Golf in the British Isles was part of my therapy, and I needed a lot of it.

For reasons I was able to understand much later, I determined I would give myself 10 years to play as many courses as I could, or until I found the peace I hoped God would grant me. Whether that meant I played only a certain number or all of the ones I included on my lists, I didn't know. At the time, the 10-year period was just an arbitrary timeframe that indirectly connected to turning 60 a decade later.

Understanding what this represented to me personally, I planned to create an informal record or journal of my days there that would also include photographs I took. I hoped, like other golf books, including Mr. Steel's, that I loved, that this personal journal would provide its own form of medicine when I wasn't there—when I struggled at home over the loss of Sally.

As friends and acquaintances heard what I was doing, they asked me to share my recollections and reflections with them about my golf and Sally. They encouraged me to write a book. It was a daunting notion, because I hadn't even been able to write a good term paper when I was in school.

Given this reality, I knew if I were to write a book, I would need help to put my story together to make it worthy of sharing with others. While playing a remote course in Ireland, God sent me a loud message about where to look for that help. I had a thought to contact Ron Green, Jr., a sportswriter with the *Charlotte Observer* specializing in golf.

After speaking with Ron and hearing his willingness to help, I began to contemplate what I would include in a book. As I traveled back and forth each year, many times more than once in the same year, I contemplated the book idea. If I did it, what would I say? How much would I share about Sally? In terms of my golf, I thought I could include a rating of the various courses I had played, a list of my favorites courses by country, as well as other lists, like my favorite places where I stayed or information about the golf course architects. I knew I could also throw in stories about events that occurred while there that were unique or worthy of sharing. But what else did I want to say? What else did I need to share?

Writing a book is a big commitment, and making the commitment to start didn't happen immediately. As each year passed and I played more courses, I kept pushing it further away. Still, I hoped that with Ron's help, I could eventually write something worthy of Sally's memory and of potential interest to those who asked me to do it. When anyone questioned me about my plans to start, I always said I needed to finish playing the courses I had on my list first.

On May 24, 2014, I played the last course on my list. Almost as soon as we walked off the green of that last hole, Jo told me it was time to start the book. I told her I wanted time to regroup at home and I would start in the fall, hoping that would satisfy her. The truth is that I remained intimidated by the prospect of writing it. I also worried that my story was not worthy of being told.

As 2014 wound down, the book idea was never far away, but I still hadn't done anything definitive about it. I hoped Jo was going to give me a pass. Wishful thinking. I should have known better after being with her for nearly 45 years.

Celebrating my 61st birthday on January 12, 2015, Jo gave me a big box with a ribbon on it. Inside were a card and a book. The book was titled, *How to Bring Your Book to Life This Year,* by Lisa Shultz and Andrea Costantine.

The card read, "No more excuses. I will get you a ghostwriter if Ron won't be able to help. Get to work!"

I looked up at her after reading the card and said, "Okay, no more excuses." I told Jo I'd contact Ron to see if he was still interested in helping and, if not, I would formulate Plan B. I knew Ron had left the *Charlotte Observer* to cover golf for *Global Golf Post,* a weekly digital magazine, and it required extensive travel. I anticipated we'd go with Plan B.

I emailed Ron. He replied, saying he'd be happy to do it, and we met for lunch to lay out a plan. We talked about several approaches and agreed it would be best for me to start writing and see where it led me.

Ron asked if I knew how I would get the book published and marketed. I didn't, but I had little doubt that everything would eventually be worked out. So much had happened in my life that I'd come to understand how things sometimes have a way of working themselves out.

On vacation in mid-February, I sat down at my computer in our room and wondered where to start. Without much thought, I knew exactly where to begin. My walk began as I sat on the curb at 4:30 a.m. on April 4, 2004, looking at the car Sally and Grace were riding in and realizing they were gone. I began writing and didn't stop until I finished on July 17, 2015, while The Open Championship was being played through the wind and rain at St. Andrews, the exact place where my love affair with links golf in the British Isles had begun in 1984.

This book is different than I ever imagined it would be. The lists that I thought this book would include never entered my mind as I wrote. They may be things to share later, but I knew this book had to be much more. It's more personal than I'd envisioned, but it had to be in order to fully share the walk I've been on. I've also come to understand that I could not have begun before I did, because I was not ready. As the thoughts and words began to flow, God revealed feelings, memories, and insights I had never seen or realized until those moments. Ultimately, I came to understand that I was not in control. He was, and had always been, the One in control.

My hope is that you find *A Long Walk with Sally* a worthy read, because I have shared far more than I ever expected. It has been a long walk indeed, but it took me until the very end to fully recognize the peace God intended for me in the aftermath of losing my sweet Sally.

TO HIM I GIVE THE GLORY!

1

Staying Safe

~~

As Sally often did, she came home from Peace College in Raleigh to spend the weekend at home. She arrived on Friday night, March 26, to have dinner with her mother and me and to spend time with friends from school and church. After their years at Charlotte Country Day School, they had all gone off to various colleges but, like Sally, many returned home on free weekends to maintain the friendships that stretched across years.

Sally loved being home, back in Iron Station, North Carolina, where she had grown up with Jo and me and her brothers, Graham and Reynolds, bringing her own sparkle to the world.

For Sally, life was a rainbow. She had a spirit that was contagious. She had a smile that made other people smile and a light that came from within. This is not *just* how I saw her. This is the way the world saw Sally. It was commonplace to have people who met or knew her tell us how much they loved being in her company. You could not be around her without feeling the warmth she radiated.

Sally's best friend from birth was her first cousin, Grace. They were the same age and had grown up together, practically sisters whose lives were wrapped together like a hair braid. Grace was a student at North Carolina State and, like Sally, often came home on weekends to spend time with her family. Many times, they rode home together.

Often on Friday nights when she got home, Jo, Sally, and I headed out to dinner, where we could catch up on all that had happened with each of us before Sally headed out to be with her friends later that night. She would share how school was going and new friends she'd made that week, and we'd tell her about anything new that might have occurred in our lives. Sally had her own life, she'd been that way for years, but her family always remained at the center. On March 26, we wound up at Mickey and Mooch in Huntersville, where we had a wonderful evening. It was the kind of evening we loved to spend together.

On Saturday morning, the three of us, along with Graham, had breakfast together at Stacy's in Denver. Afterwards, I headed to Charlotte to play at Quail Hollow while Jo and Sally went shopping for clothes. That night Sally headed out to meet up with friends in Cornelius while Jo and I stayed home with Graham. She told us she would spend the night with one of her friends and would see us in the morning after church.

After spending time with her friends, she decided not to stay overnight and came home. She arrived back at our house at 3:00 a.m. on Sunday and woke us to tell us she had arrived—reassuring words to parents with children of any age. However, knowing she was out on the road by herself at that hour of the night concerned us.

The next day, before Sally headed back to Raleigh, I told her that, while we trusted her driving in the middle of the night, it was the other drivers that worried us. I told her what my mother had told me—nothing good happens after 11:00 p.m. I also called on the late comedian Richard Pryor to help make my point. He had done a great monologue in the '70s about hanging around street corners with his friends late at night. When Pryor asked his friends what they were waiting for, one of them said, "11:30, because we're going to pitch a bitch at 11:30!" My point to Sally was that her mother and I would rather she not be driving late at night. As long as she felt safe where she was, we preferred she spend the night there.

One week later, our world was torn apart. My sweet Sally never made it home that April night.

2

Please Sally…

The last time I talked with Sally was around 12:30 a.m. on April 4 when, remembering our conversation a week earlier about being on the road late at night, she called and asked, "Dad, I'd like to come home so I can go to the eight-thirty Palm Sunday service at Grace Covenant. Grace and a friend from school want to come with me too."

Earlier that evening, she'd had dinner with her best friend at Country Day, Kasey Pryor, and Kasey's family. Sally then met up with Grace to head to their brothers, who were enrolled at UNCC, to watch the NCAA basketball semifinals. They had planned to spend the night there and return home the next day before heading back to Raleigh.

Sally's faith and her commitment to church were fundamental to her life. They were guiding lights for her and, understanding that, I told her it was okay to come home. I then reminded her to be careful and to wake Jo and me when she arrived. The drive normally took about 30 minutes.

At 1:35 a.m., Jo awoke and realized Sally wasn't home. She woke me, and I immediately called Sally's cell phone. The call went directly to her voicemail.

"Hey, this is Sally. Please leave a message and I will call you back."

I didn't want to leave a message. I wanted to hear Sally talk to me. I left her the message, "Sug, this is Dad. Please give me a call to let us know where you are."

Rather than wait for Sally to call us, Jo and I dressed, got into our car, and went out to find her. We drove toward Birkdale, north of Charlotte, because Jo remembered that Sally's friend lived near there. As we drove east from our home on Highway 73, we kept calling Sally's phone. It kept going to voicemail. With each unanswered call, I began to say out loud, "Sally, please answer your phone. Please Sug, answer it."

As we passed the intersection of Catawba Avenue and Highway 73, about a quarter of a mile further, we saw a Huntersville police car blocking the road at the crest of the upcoming hill. I felt my heart sink.

"Oh dear God, please don't let this be them," I said.

When we crested the hill and reached the police officer, we were staring at a sea of emergency vehicles with flashing lights a half a mile below us. Something terrible had happened, but we could not see the vehicles involved.

I rolled down the window and told the officer our daughter was late coming home and we thought she may have come this way. She was driving a blue BMW and we believed she would be with two other girls. I'll never forget the officer's eyes as he took a long, painful look at us before he walked away to use his police radio.

When the officer returned, he said the accident involved a Chevrolet Blazer with one male occupant and a white Honda with three young girls. For a moment, I felt a sense of relief. Sally would have been driving her BMW. My next thought, however, erased that momentary reprieve. *But there were three girls in the white Honda—three girls that could be Sally, Grace, and Sally's friend.* Since Grace drove a Mitsubishi Eclipse, I knew it wasn't her car in the accident. Unfortunately, I didn't know what her friend drove. *Maybe, by the grace of God, they are still on their way home.*

I asked the officer how serious the accident was, and he didn't give me a direct answer. He said he'd find out and let us know. But I could tell by the anguished look in his eyes that he knew more than he was saying. Hoping the girls had gone to Grace's house rather than ours, Jo called her sister Anne. Anne and Grace's father, Dick, had divorced a few years earlier and, when she was home, Grace stayed with her mother. Anne said that the girls weren't there and she hadn't talked to Grace since much earlier in the evening. After hanging up with Jo, Anne called Grace and, not getting an answer, called Jo back and said she'd come to meet us.

A sense of despair and hopelessness began to take hold of us. Jo suggested we pray and we did, asking God that our girls might be safe and that the people involved in the accident were okay. It was a desperate prayer by parents who feared the worst. When Jo finished our prayer, we sat silently in our car, staring out at the emergency lights as they lit up the worst night of our lives. We waited for the officer to come back, terrified of what he might say to us. We prayed that one of our phones would ring and it would be our sweet Sally telling us she was okay.

3

Our Worst Fears

~⌣~

It was my worst fear, our worst fear, a parent's horror. A recurring nightmare of mine was becoming real. As Jo and I sat in our car, we realized the world we'd known had come to a standstill. When we finished praying, we knew we were caught in a horrible reality. In the absence of a call from Sally or word that she was okay, we felt we had to wait to see if the heartbreaking scene in front of us included Sally, Grace, and their friend. For nearly an hour we sat in our Suburban, staring out the windshield, waiting for word and wishing for a miracle. The police officer stood silently beside our car. The longer we sat there, the more real the feeling became that Sally was not going to call us—our phones were not going to ring with her sweet voice on the other end telling us everything was fine.

There were so many lights and so few answers. No one would talk to us. Later, we would learn that law enforcement was processing the accident as a crime scene, chronicling the heartbreaking details while we sat in quiet agony. At approximately 4:30 a.m., a police car drove out from within the vehicles crowded around the accident and pulled up next to us. A non-uniformed officer asked us to follow him in our vehicle.

I will never be able to erase the memory of the ride down the hill. Jo and I held hands without saying a word. Anne and a friend followed us in another car. When we stopped, the scene was awash in bright lights mounted atop fire trucks and other emergency vehicles. Near the southeast corner of the intersection was a white Honda with its right side destroyed. A sheet was draped over the car. As we got out of our car, another non-uniformed officer met us, and he spoke with compassion.

"I'm sorry but we believe your daughters were riding in that car. The drivers of both vehicles have been transported to the hospital, and we know their names. However, the two girls riding with the driver of the Honda did not make it. They are still in the car but neither had identification with them. To be sure, we need you to confirm they're your daughters."

As the officer told us this and looked at me, my knees buckled. Another officer grabbed my arm to keep me from collapsing.

"Sir, I can't," I said, barely able to speak. "I don't want this to be my final memory of my daughter."

Anne couldn't speak. With strength and courage only God could provide from her resolute faith in Him, Jo said, "I will do it."

The police helped me to the curb, and through the blur of what was happening, I watched with both awe and heartbreak as two officers walked Jo to the car. When they raised the sheet, I covered my face with my hands. I couldn't look. Sally and Grace were gone. The reality was setting in.

I wanted to cry but I couldn't. I began to blame myself. Just a week ago I had told her to stay where she was if it was late and she felt safe. If she didn't feel safe, I told her to call me. I would always come and get her. *If only.* It was a thought that would haunt me for quite some time.

When I looked up, Jo was coming toward me, flanked by the two officers who had taken her to the car. She was walking without assistance. I didn't need her to tell me what she'd seen. The look on her face said everything. It was Sally and Grace in the car.

"It's our girls," Jo said as she began to cry. The officer who was next to me helped me to stand up, and I hugged Jo. Nearby, Anne was held by a friend.

I asked the officers what had happened and was told that because the investigation was ongoing, they were not at liberty to share any details. I was stunned. We had just identified our dead daughter and our niece and they wouldn't tell us what had happened. I was trying to process a nightmare and not getting any help from the law enforcement on site. When we were then told that the girls' bodies would be taken to the coroner's office and held until the investigation was complete, I panicked and became even more confused.

"Why?" I asked. "They were just riding in the car. They had nothing to do with what happened."

I pleaded not to take our girls to the morgue. The officer kept his composure, although it didn't seem easy for him to do. He responded that it had to be done this way. He instructed us further that we needed to go home and wait for a phone call telling us what to do next. After taking our phone number, he offered to have an officer drive us home.

I stood there feeling helpless, confused, and unimaginably sad. I had no control over what was happening. I wanted to do something, but there was nothing we could do. In shock, Jo and I walked to our car and drove home. Anne and her friend headed to her home. All of us heartbroken beyond belief.

4

We Need Help

I don't remember the ride home. Our world had been torn apart. A few hours earlier, we were happy and laughing. Now Sally and Grace were gone. The enormity of this thought was too much for me to fully comprehend.

At home, I said to Jo, "We need help but I don't know who to call."

Who do you call at such a moment?

Earlier that evening, we'd had dinner with Greg and Jennifer Currie, and we decided to call them. It was as if God's hand was at work, leading us to call the Curries. I called Greg at approximately 5:30 a.m. When Greg answered, I put together the words as best I could.

"Greg, Sally and Grace were killed last night in a car accident and Jo and I need your help. Could you come to our home?" I asked.

They would be on their way immediately, Greg said. Within an hour, Greg and Jennifer were at our house. As I walked to the front door to meet the Curries, I looked up to our second floor to

Sally's bedroom. The thoughts of her never bounding downstairs again or me never again hearing her sweet voice coming from her room hit me hard. She was gone. How could I ever come to terms with this reality?

Not long after the Curries got to our home, close friends Ronny and Susan Brown arrived. Jo and I were frantic. We were still waiting for answers, and the thought of the girls being at the coroner's office consumed me. I couldn't stand the idea and asked Greg to help me make sure that didn't happen. I was shutting down. I couldn't handle anything. I was in shock. My life was becoming a blur and I felt destroyed. My world shattered. I couldn't comprehend that my sweet Sally was gone.

Greg took charge. He began making calls, working to get whatever information he could, and doing everything possible to have the girls' bodies released as soon as possible.

Our sons, Reynolds and Graham, still didn't know what had happened. They had been away the previous night. I called Reynolds, got his voicemail, and requested that he call me immediately. Graham had spent the night with a friend, so I called there. I talked to the mother of Graham's friend and, as best as I could, told her what had happened. I asked if Graham could stay a while longer and that they not let him see the news while we decided how best to tell him.

When Reynolds returned my call, I told him about the girls. He'd been on his first date with a girl he'd met that week, and they had watched the basketball games together before he got back to his apartment. He knew Sally and Grace had been heading home on Saturday night, because Sally had called him. Reynolds was devastated. He could not speak. We learned later that the girl he'd gone out with, Jennifer Tingen, had lost her teenage brother, Justin, two years earlier.

Later that day, we called the family Graham had stayed with and asked them to bring him home. I will never forget Graham's face as he exited their car and saw all the cars in our drive, obviously wondering what was going on. Jo and I met him at the door and told him about Sally and Grace. He had come home smiling after spending the weekend with one of his closest friends only to be told his sister had been killed in a car wreck. He was suddenly a little boy again, realizing the sister he loved was gone, and he cried uncontrollably.

I wanted to do something for both boys to protect them from this heartbreak, but there was nothing to be done. We were all emotionally destroyed. As the realization of what had happened settled over Jo and me, it took its toll.

Around 9:00 a.m., Greg pulled Jo and me aside. He had made several calls and wanted to update us on what was happening. The police, Greg said, were required to conduct a thorough investigation, which was the reason they could not discuss any details or release the girls' bodies immediately. He had spoken to the police chief of Huntersville and the Mecklenburg County district attorney. The car the girls were in had been broadsided by another vehicle traveling approximately 90 miles per hour. Sally had been in the front passenger seat with her seatbelt on, sitting exactly where the other car had smashed into the Honda. Grace had been in the backseat behind Sally, and because she hadn't been wearing a seatbelt, she was thrown to the other side of the car. It was believed that the driver of the vehicle that hit them had been under the influence of alcohol. There were still more details to be obtained, and Greg promised that he would share everything as he learned more. He added that since they'd now finished the initial part of their investigation, the girls could be released immediately.

Again, the same thought returned—why hadn't I told Sally to stay where she was? Why hadn't I gone to get the girls? It was my fault.

Greg also told us we needed to make some decisions about who would pick up the girls and what kind of funeral arrangements needed to be made. "It's time," he said, "to think about writing an obituary." It was too much for me. I couldn't imagine writing Sally's obituary. She had just been here, so full of life. I sat motionless while Jo called Anne with the update. Friends came by to console us, and many of them needed consoling as well. Losing a child is a devastating loss for everyone. I still hadn't been able to cry. I wanted to, but the tears wouldn't come.

I continued to marvel at Jo's strength. She was as heartbroken as I, but she wasn't emotionally paralyzed the way I was. I wilted. She drew strength and guidance from her deep faith. Jo and Greg talked details. I just sat there. We needed to call someone to pick up the girls, and I immediately thought of L.D. "Bud" Warlick, owner of Warlick's Funeral Home. Bud and his wife, Molly, had lost their young son on a beach trip, and I called him, trusting in his compassion and empathy. Molly answered the phone, and when I identified myself, she said, "David, I am so sorry. We saw the horrible news about Sally and Grace this morning." She handed the phone to Bud who expressed his condolences and offered to help in any way he could. "Please," I asked him, "send someone to get the girls in Charlotte as soon as possible."

As we ended our call, Bud said to me, "David, there is nothing worse than losing a child, but it does get better." I couldn't answer him. I still couldn't accept that Sally was gone. Get better? How could it?

Jo was with Greg and several friends. Paul Turbedsky, the youth minister from Grace Covenant, had arrived. Because it was Palm

Sunday, the other clergy were busy with services, but Paul, knowing Sally through her involvement in the youth ministry, had come to be with us.

"We need to decide what to do with the girls' remains," Jo said.

It was too much to think about. Jo said she wanted the girls cremated. I just sat there speechless.

"David," Jo said, "we have to make these decisions. I have discussed this with Paul and he assures me this will have no bearing on their souls and their Heavenly appearance. I can only tell you how I saw Sally in the car. This is what we must do."

One of the few things I had noticed while sitting on the curb was the absence of skid marks. My heart still aches at that thought. I can't imagine what Jo saw when she reached that car. Her strength and courage sheltered me from a memory I could not have handled.

I looked desperately at Paul.

"David, the girls are fine," he said. "They are now with their Heavenly Father and you've got to trust that. What Jo is telling you is correct and I believe she is making the right decision."

I nodded my acceptance. I couldn't speak. If I could have walked out the door and kept going, I would have. Sitting on the curb at the accident site, I had been overwhelmed by the desire to walk. Where, I didn't know, but away from the unbearable heartbreak.

We needed to plan a memorial service. It was Holy Week, with all the attendant services. After considering the options, we decided to hold a visitation at our home on Monday night with the memorial service Tuesday at Grace Covenant. Again, I just wanted to walk away. When Greg told me I had to write Sally's obituary, I did walk away. The thought of writing your child's obituary plumbs the depths of sadness. I couldn't do it. Greg came and put his arm around my shoulder.

"I can only imagine what you're going through," Greg said when he found me. "But we need your help on this. We need to let people know the arrangements. We've talked to the editor of the *Charlotte Observer* and they're holding up finalization of the paper until they receive this."

Where do you start? Again, Jo remained remarkably strong and calm as we went through the details of Sally's life. Anne and Dick agreed to a joint visitation and memorial, a recognition of their enduring friendship. Their remains would be placed together. My parents are interred in a family plot at Machpelah Church, a small historic church not far from our home. I believed they would want their granddaughter near them and decided to have them placed there.

Early in the afternoon, Greg had more to share about what had happened. Sally and Grace were riding with a young girl named Suzanne Kessler, who also went to Peace College. Her grandparents lived in the Birkdale neighborhood just off Interstate 77 near Huntersville, and it appeared they were going to their home and were making a left-hand turn at the intersection. Suzanne had suffered significant injuries and had to be cut out of the car but was expected to make a full recovery. The driver of the vehicle that hit them was named David Scott Shimp. He was also at the hospital but was not seriously injured. The DA's office was reviewing the case and would be making a decision on filing charges sometime in the near future.

As I continued to process this, I kept thinking about why I hadn't gone to get them or asked Sally to stay, as I had suggested the weekend before. *I could have kept this from happening. They were riding in a car trying to come home. Both drivers who caused this are going to live but Sally and Grace are now gone. It's my fault.*

That evening, close friends and neighbors, Randy and Dianne Dorton, came over. Randy was the chief engineer for Hendrick Motorsports NASCAR teams, and they had just returned from the race in Texas. Someone had pulled him aside to let him know about the accident. The Dortons knew both girls well and were heartbroken. For the next week, Randy set aside all his responsibilities with Hendrick to help in any way he could.

We finally went to our bedroom around 10, but there was no rest. How could there be when our lives were in pieces?

5

A Special Part of Me

~

Monday, April 5, 2004

The first day of life without Sally.

How can this be? I still cannot accept that she is gone. I was jolted to reality when asked that I help put together the service for Sally and Grace the next day. There was music to pick and scripture readings to choose. Again, I simply could not function. Jo, however, continued to show unimaginable courage and strength. She mentioned that Sally had recently listened to a new artist named Josh Groban who had an amazing voice. She loved one song in particular. I didn't know anything about Josh Groban, but Jo felt the song needed to be part of the service. Someone located his most recent CD *Closer* and played the song "You Raise Me Up." As I listened to the song, my heart broke all over again. All I could do was think of Sally. *God, please help me.*

Trying to focus, I remembered a service I had attended the year before for the father of one of my best friends from Chapel Hill. I was struck by the music his family had chosen to sing, one song in particular. It was one of the most moving Christian hymns I'd ever heard, and for that reason I had kept the bulletin. Something I had never done before. I couldn't remember the name of the song, and when I found the bulletin in my chest of drawers, I couldn't breathe. It was called "Here I Am, Lord."

We completed the plan for the service. I was filled with nothing but awe for her strength when Jo said she wanted to speak and to read from the New Testament. Grace's brother Christopher also wanted to speak. They had unbelievable strength that God did not bestow on me. Greg continued to handle one difficult task after another on our behalf. God bless him, I can only imagine what he found himself confronted with during the hours and days that followed our call for help.

As the day unfolded, the local television stations and newspapers wanted a statement from our family or to have the opportunity to speak with someone. One of the television stations also asked to fly over our home during the visitation that would take place in the evening. We asked them all to respect our privacy and in due course we would have something to say, but not yet. To their credit, all honored our request and maintained a distance.

Greg stayed in touch with both the district attorney's office and the Huntersville police, gathering more details regarding the accident. Based on the police investigation, while the official results had not been obtained and were being sent to Raleigh, it was believed Shimp's blood alcohol level was at least two times the legal amount. Based on that and his speed, he would be charged with two counts of second-degree murder. I was numb. While knowing that on occasion I'd had more than my share to drink and had probably exceeded the legal limit, my reaction was always to drive more responsibly and make my way carefully home, even in my youth. But to drive at nearly 90 miles per hour? Why? The answer would come later, we presumed.

Greg and my brother Walter understood the challenge of getting our family from our house to Grace Covenant the next day during midday traffic, especially with the number of people who would be going to the church. Word had also gotten back to us that a massive memorial was being assembled at the intersection where the girls' car had come to rest. I did not want to drive by there and asked if we could find another route. Greg and Walter went to work to figure something out.

Through the coordination of three law enforcement departments—Lincoln County Sheriff's Department, the Cornelius Police Department, and the Huntersville Police Department—our procession would be allowed to avoid the accident scene. Their effort touched my heart.

Later that day, a neighbor came by and told us that Suzanne's grandparents and mother wanted to come by if we would allow them. Even though we were still trying to understand what had taken place, we knew they had also suffered a tremendous blow and thought it was appropriate to meet them. Their visit turned out to be something neither of us expected. While we learned that the girls were heading to their home so Suzanne could get what she planned to wear to Palm Sunday service, to our disbelief, most of what they wanted to talk about was that their child was going to be okay and how relieved and elated they were at this news. They were almost euphoric. Without question, if Sally had made it, I would have felt the same way. However, neither of us would have been able to take this mood into the home of the family suffering the worst blow imaginable.

An hour before the visitation was to begin, while everyone was busy getting ready, I went to Sally's bedroom to be alone. She loved her bedroom, and everywhere I looked I saw Sally. On the chaise lounge near the window were clothes she'd brought home for the weekend. On the floor was a pair of her shoes. On her chest of drawers were pictures of her friends. I lay on her bed trying to feel her presence, asking God to help me. I did not want to accept that the nightmare I was experiencing was indeed reality and that she would never be coming home again. The voices downstairs preparing our home for the visitation told me it was indeed true.

That evening we held the visitation. I remember little about it or who came. I wish I did. I know many were suffering along with us. While we expected a large number of people, we never imagined that so many people would come. Greg told me later that the line to enter our neighborhood reached three miles, prompting the sheriff's department to dispatch deputies to manage the traffic. In their 19 short years, Sally and Grace had touched many.

The visitation time had to be extended. We knew it was important to let those who came have the opportunity to speak to us. Along with Grace's family, we stayed until the last person had spoken to us around 11:00 p.m. I remember Sally's friends congregating in our backyard, so many of them crying. Like us, they were heartbroken and devastated. Sadly, this wasn't new to them. Sally's death was not the first loss of a friend nor would it be the last. They had lost another classmate two years earlier in an auto accident. Tragically, their class would lose another member that summer in another auto accident.

Tuesday, April 6, 2004

The saddest day of my life was the day the girls' memorial service was held. I remember little about the morning, other than beginning to accept the reality of Sally being gone. Little else mattered.

At 11:00 a.m., we began our trip to Grace Covenant for the one o'clock service. Greg and Walter had arranged for several large limousines to transport our families and friends who had been by our side since Sunday. It was another demonstration of their wonderful efforts to accommodate us and allow us to grieve. I don't remember much about the ride except that we thankfully avoided driving by the location of the accident. It would be several months before I would find the strength to go there.

Making our way to the pew, I saw that the church was crowded with people who were crying. I also noticed a number of uniformed police officers and firemen. I later learned that they were the ones who had been at the accident site. I stared at a blank wall to avoid making eye contact with anyone or seeing a picture of Sally or Grace. I was afraid of breaking down. It would be months before I could look at a picture of Sally.

Jo chose to read Ephesians 6, verses 10-18, known as the armor of God, while Christopher chose Psalm 23. One of the few recollections I have from the service is seeing first Christopher and then Jo walk to the front of the church to read what they had chosen with immense composure and grace. They had incredible strength. Jo told me the day before as we planned the service that she wanted to do it for Sally and Grace and she refused to allow her emotions to overwhelm her. I'm sure Christopher felt the same.

Their demonstration of incredible strength and grace reminded me of my father at my mother's funeral service in 1991. My father had been almost entirely paralyzed from the neck down as a result of an auto accident in 1989 after another driver rear-ended him. When we arrived at Machpelah for her graveside service and were preparing his wheelchair for him, to our amazement and awe, he told my two brothers and me that he would walk to the gravesite. He said he had to do it for her. We were stunned. He'd had minimal movement in his legs since the accident. No one said a word. With the help of a walker, he willed his legs to move and he made it to his chair. God grants us gifts, and this was clearly one of them. My father never walked again and passed away in 1997.

Following the church service for Sally and Grace, the procession headed for Machpelah. As our procession made its way, I was struck by the efforts of the various police departments to get us there unimpeded. Traffic was stopped so that we could proceed. Many officers stood out of their cars with their hats off and heads bowed. I was deeply moved by their actions. I'm sure many of them had children and were struggling with the thought of losing their own.

After the graveside service, many people came to our home and stayed there through the day. They didn't want to leave. It was a time to grieve together. As the day drew to a close, we returned to Machpelah with those who had stayed. We held hands and prayed together.

As we formed a circle around where the girls' ashes were placed below my parents and I saw the tears of the others, I began to fully comprehend that we had lost our sweet Sally and beloved niece Grace. The sun was setting as we held hands and cried. Watching it settle below the horizon, I had no idea where my life would go from here. I had just turned 50, and my life had been blessed in many ways. I had so much to be thankful for up to this moment. Standing there with our friends and family, I began to reflect on my life and my sweet Sally, her life, and what she meant to me. With her passing, I realized I had lost a special part of me. Whether the sun would ever shine again for the rest of my life, I had no idea. My world was now in full freefall with no bottom in sight. It was the saddest moment of my life, yet I still could not cry.

6

One Lucky Baby

~

I was born to some of the greatest parents a child could have. I was the oldest of four children and blessed in so many ways.

My mother, Kathryn King Goode, was affectionately known as Kappy. Her father was one of the Southeast's most successful construction contractors and developers for more than 40 years, starting in the 1930s. They lived in Charlotte and had a prominent place in the community. My mother was one of the most beautiful ladies of her day and was frequently photographed for the fashion pages of numerous newspapers and magazines. Beyond her outward beauty, my mother was even more beautiful as a person.

My father, David Clark, Sr., was born into one of the state's more prominent political families and had the good fortune to be financially successful. He grew up in Lincolnton, North Carolina, flew in the Pacific theatre during World War II, and then returned to North Carolina to become a well-respected and successful attorney, businessman, and politician in his own right. He was known as a gentleman and man of the utmost integrity.

After finishing law school at Chapel Hill, he chose to practice law in his hometown when he was not in public office. Lincolnton was like something from a Norman Rockwell painting—a peaceful, happy small town where no one locked their doors and kids played outside freely.

My parents

Besides his family, my father's greatest love was our farm in eastern Lincoln County. Over more than 30 years, he assembled nearly 6,000 acres, starting with the purchase of a beautiful historic home called Ingleside. As children, we would often go there on weekends to spend the day with him as he made the rounds, checking on the property and meeting with the man who oversaw the upkeep of the farm. In the summer, we would play in its many creeks and fish in the ponds my father had built.

My father, President Kennedy,
and Governor Terry Sanford

Ingleside

In the late 1960s, we moved as a family to Ingleside from Lincolnton. My childhood was like growing up in a dream.

My family in the summer of 1972

Though my two brothers, Allison and Walter, my sister, Caroline, and I could not be more different, we love and respect each other and remain close.

My father learned golf in his youth at Lincoln Country Club, a nine-hole course in those days. My mother's family had a membership at Charlotte Country Club where she played on occasion with friends. However, after marrying my father, my mother became an avid golfer. They made regular springtime trips to the Masters, and I remember their stories about seeing Arnie and Jack. My mother, it seemed, had a crush on Gary Player. My parents were taken with Player's commitment to physical fitness, and each morning my father would do push-ups, sit-ups, and stretching.

My parents introduced me to golf at age five. We spent part of our summers in Blowing Rock, where we had a home. That was where they decided I should learn the game they loved. They set up a series of lessons with a female assistant pro. While I don't remember much about the beginner lessons, I do remember her teaching me how to grip the club with the proper overlap grip. While I changed it a few years ago to an interlocking grip, I remember it as the lesson for a lifetime.

It was my grandfather, Thorne McKenzie Clark, who had the most influence on my early days as a golfer. Pop, as we called him, loved the game with a passion. As president of a local bank he started, Pop had every Wednesday afternoon and weekends off. On occasion Pop would take me to the local nine-hole course, where we would play with a man from the bank and the school superintendent. Pop had a set of PowerBilt woods, a set of MacGregor Tourney irons, and a Bullseye putter. I coveted those clubs, and I still have his driver and bag.

Later in life, Pop developed cataracts and nearly lost his sight, but that didn't keep him from playing golf. He would have his playing partners help him to his ball, select his club, and align him properly. That's how he played.

Like most kids of my generation, I loved playing different sports with my friends at school and in our neighborhood. Growing up, we played outside most of the time. Football, baseball, kickball, basketball. We played them all. Summers, though, I gave myself over to golf. In the mornings, I would either walk to the nine-hole course or have my parents drop me around eight o'clock. I would play as much as I wanted, then head to the pool before going home, where we'd find something else to do in the evening. It was a storybook childhood.

While I played golf at my high school, East Lincoln, and managed to be named the team's MVP my senior year, my interest in golf remained primarily a summer passion. I was a good player but not exceptional. Football became my emphasis, where I was a solid cornerback, good enough to have received letters from several small regional colleges inquiring about my potential interest in playing football for them.

During the third game in my senior season, I sustained a knee injury that required major surgery and ended my season. I assumed it would also end any ideas I had of playing college football. My lifelong best friend, John Lawing, was an all-state quarterback at Lincolnton High and was being heavily recruited by many major schools. He initially signed a letter of intent with North Carolina to play under Bill Dooley. The Tar Heels coach loved to take some of the best high school quarterbacks and convert them to defensive back.

John was aware of Dooley's tendency, and when Coach Cal Stoll left Wake Forest to become head coach at Minnesota, while we were still high school seniors, it changed both of our plans. Stoll called John and offered him a full scholarship, telling John he would be the Gophers' starting quarterback. It was a chance to play football in the Big Ten.

The thought of being so far from home weighed on John, and he told Coach Stoll that he would seriously consider it if Minnesota would consider giving me a chance to play football. To be sure, this had nothing to do with my playing ability and everything to do with John. My skill set was not major school worthy. After John gave me a heads up, I got a call from Coach Stoll, who offered me the opportunity to try out for the team and the possibility of a scholarship if I made it. He then offered to fly us up for a school visit and the chance to see if we would like to attend there.

Several weeks later, a private jet owned by a big Minnesota booster picked us up in Charlotte. As recruiting visits go, I would say this one ranked up there, so much so, the school ended up in hot water with NCAA several years later for multiple recruiting infractions. However, it sold us, particularly John, on the idea of playing at Minnesota, and he signed a national letter of intent.

In August, we headed off to Minneapolis for the start of football practice. During the first team meeting, I looked at the players around me. They were bigger and better than me. I weighed 190 pounds but didn't look nor feel like a Big Ten football player, especially when I looked at so many solid 200-pound guys. What had I been thinking? I knew immediately that I was in over my head. The most I could hope for would be to make the travel squad—if I survived the physical challenge of practice against my teammates.

I told Coach Stoll and John that there was no reason for me to continue, and they understood. Still, I wanted to stay at Minnesota to support John and experience life in a different part of the country. I felt I owed it to John to be there with him, although my thoughts had already begun to shift from football to golf. John started at quarterback most of his freshman season and had a reasonably good year, until he severely dislocated his shoulder in the final home game of the season.

I flew home for Thanksgiving, and when I flew back to Minnesota, I arrived in a driving snowstorm. I wouldn't see the ground again until March. That wasn't new to the natives of Minnesota, but it was a grim, cold reminder to me that I wasn't in North Carolina anymore. I endured more subzero days and nights in one week than I had during my entire 18 years of life in Lincoln County. Walking to class early in the morning was brutal. At every opportunity, I used the tunnels around campus to get from building to building. Eventually, the snow melted and spring arrived. I signed up for intramural golf, and that's where my passion for the game really began to blossom.

At home for the summer, I headed to Cowan's Ford Country Club near Lake Norman and fell into the routine of my youth. I didn't want to *just* play golf, though. I wanted to improve, so I worked at my game throughout the summer on the practice range. In addition, to our family's membership at Cowan's Ford, we were also members of Quail Hollow Club, Grandfather Golf and Country Club, Linville Golf Club, and the Country Club of North Carolina, four of the most prestigious clubs in a golf-rich state. It couldn't have been better for someone with a growing passion for a sport.

When it came time to return to Minnesota for my sophomore year, I didn't want to go. I considered my options for transferring, preferably to North Carolina. But I had made a commitment to John and didn't want to negatively impact his football career. I didn't realize, though, that John's situation was about to change.

Coach Stoll had signed a high school quarterback star named Tony Dungy, the man who would go on to coach the Indianapolis Colts to a Super Bowl title. John and Tony competed for the starting job that year, which John initially won. However, John was plagued most of the season by his shoulder and Tony became the preferred quarterback. At the end of season, it was clear Tony would be the starting quarterback going into next season.

As winter approached, I knew I didn't want to endure another one. I told John I would transfer as soon as I was accepted at a school somewhere in North Carolina, hopefully Carolina. He was disappointed but understood. He would remain in Minnesota, hoping to regain his starting position on the football team.

At home over Thanksgiving, I called Jo Foreman and asked her out. She was a freshman at UNC-Charlotte and had moved with her family to Lincoln County from Charlotte when I was a high school junior. We dated during high school but never developed a strong interest in one another. At the time, we seemed to have little in common. However, by anyone's standard, Jo was one of the most beautiful girls anywhere, and I decided to give things one more chance. It was then that our lives became permanently connected, for which I felt immensely lucky. We began dating regularly when I came home for Christmas, and it finalized my decision to say goodbye to Minnesota. It was an easy decision. One place was cold and snowy. The other warm, green most of the year with plenty of great golf courses, and someone I was intensely in love with.

The combination of shoulder problems and Tony Dungy's firm grip on the quarterback job led John to decide to transfer to North Carolina as well. John had also become disillusioned with college football and its all-encompassing, 12-month nature. He also missed his high school sweetheart, Vonde Cherry, who was attending school at North Carolina.

In Chapel Hill, I pledged Beta Theta Pi fraternity and quickly developed friendships for a lifetime. I found a great group of guys with nicknames such as Chico, Sturgis, Big Man, Asa, and Clement. Among the things we shared was a love of golf. One of our fraternity brothers had the shortest backswing known to man but still managed to hit it past us, which bothered us to no end. They were friendships made in Heaven, and given my parents' various club memberships, "road trip" became a part of our vernacular. Oh, the stories we could tell.

Jo was a lifeguard at Cowan's Ford during the summer, and I visited her there as often as possible, though I also had to attend summer school due to the road trips that negatively impacted my grades. When home, I'd hang around the pool while she worked. Jo also developed an interest in golf and, unlike me, had a great natural swing. After the pool closed or when she wasn't working, she would join me on the range or we'd head out to play.

The initial spark that ignited my interest in links golf occurred while attending summer school in 1975. I remember sitting in the Beta house watching Tom Watson win his first Open Championship at Carnoustie. I was struck by how different the course looked from the ones I played regularly. I listened intently to the commentators describe the difference in playing links golf versus the golf we play in the States. I was fascinated by what I saw and hoped that someday I would make my way there to play.

After finally finishing at Chapel Hill in 1978, two years later than I should have finished, I was offered a management position at Wachovia Bank in Raleigh and then Rocky Mount, North Carolina. I have great memories of those days and met some wonderful people there. I could have made a career working with the bank; however, in 1980 my parents asked me to return to Lincolnton to

become involved in our family's real estate business. Given certain family concerns, I decided to move back. It's a decision I have never regretted. Life has a way of putting you where you need to be. Coming home was one of those times.

Jo and I were married on February 20, 1982. The best day of my life.

Our first child, David Reynolds, was born July 25, 1983. As all parents would agree, there is no greater joy than the arrival of a child. God's greatest gift to humanity is the promise of eternal life through the death and resurrection of His Son, Jesus Christ. His second greatest gift is the blessing of children. At their arrival, especially your first, you fully understand and willingly accept that life will never be the same and your priorities are forever redefined. Your responsibility to your family is now above all else. As would be the case with all three of our children, I gave him a nickname that day. He was my "Sport."

Beyond Reynolds' arrival, my decision to become involved in our family business created escalating demands on my time. Golf understandably took a backseat behind both, but I continued to hold on to my hope of traveling to Scotland to play on a links course.

That fall, I suggested to Jo that we take a summer trip to the United Kingdom as a break for us both. Jo was bearing the brunt of raising Reynolds, since my work required me to travel practically every week to manage the family's real estate holdings. I admit, though, that I also hoped to play at least one round of golf on a links course to finally get a taste of what I'd seen on television.

During the spring of 1984, we found out Jo was carrying our second child. We decided to still make the trip to the UK in late June, since her due date was not until December. A travel agent made our arrangements, and I asked him to book me a round of golf on a links course at some point during our itinerary. Not being a golfer, the travel agent booked me on the Kings Course at Gleneagles, a venerable Scottish course but not a true links. It was a heathland course, located near the middle of Scotland, far from the windblown courses near the sea that I imagined myself playing.

We flew to London and headed north toward Inverness, blindly trusting our travel agent's planning. Midway through our trip, we stayed not far from Gleneagles, where I was scheduled to play. The day before my tee time, I noticed that St. Andrews was just an hour away, and I suggested to Jo that we make the drive over. I wanted to see the Old Course, the famous clubhouse, and the old gray town, and also experience where I had watched Nicklaus win The Open Championship in 1978. Plus, The Open was returning to the Old Course in 1984. As we approached St. Andrews from the west along the A91, the Royal & Ancient's clubhouse slowly came into view with the town in the background. Seeing the course with the grandstands already in place for The Open, I was mesmerized. For several hours, Jo and I wandered through the town, falling under its unique spell. The sense of history was overwhelming.

The only disappointment came when we walked to the par-4 17th hole—the famous Road Hole—and saw the Old Course Hotel. On such a special spot, it was one of the ugliest structures I had ever seen. It seemed so out of character with its ancient and enchanting surroundings.

About 400 yards away, the feeling was completely different as we stood next to the St. Andrews Woolen Mill overlooking the 18th green, the clubhouse, and the bleachers. It's one thing to see it on television. It's something else to see it for yourself, to feel the air, and sense the centuries of golf that have been played there. It's almost spiritual if you have golf in your soul.

Over dinner that night, I realized playing one round at Gleneagles wasn't going to satisfy me. I now had a fire inside to really experience links golf. With another child on the way, I knew I had to be tactful when I told Jo, "I'm really enjoying our time here together and I think I'll skip playing tomorrow. However, if you're okay with it, I'd like to come back sometime and play with a group of guys. I'm not sure when, but sometime." Jo, without hesitation, said that would be fine.

From there, we headed north to the Scottish Highlands, to The Tulchan Lodge on the River Spey, ground zero for single malt scotch and some of the best salmon fishing in the world. I was oblivious to the greatness to which I was being introduced. We spent three of the most memorable nights of our marriage there, and I first tasted single malt whisky. It wasn't love at first taste, but I realized I could grow to like good single malts.

In Edinburgh before our flight to London, I remembered a course south of town called Gullane, where Lee Trevino had won The Open Championship. We rode to Gullane, found the course, and parked. We got out, and I remember looking across the 10th hole thinking, "Oh my." There was no doubt I would return.

Back home, I watched Seve Ballesteros beat Tom Watson for the '84 Open Championship, and I put myself there, remembering how we'd stood beside the Old Course's 18th green just weeks earlier. It was an overwhelming feeling, and I thought, "How did I miss this all these years?" While unsure when, I knew I wanted to find my way back to play the Old Course and other true links courses as soon as I could.

That December, God blessed us again with the arrival of our second child, a beautiful little girl.

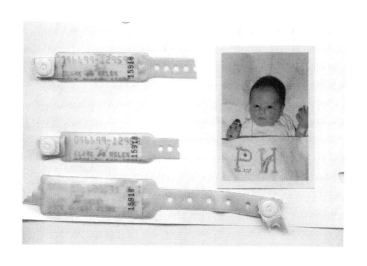

7

My Sweet Sally

Sally McKenzie Clark was born December 9, 1984, with a smile on her little face. Most newborns arrive crying. Not Sally. In her first moments, Sally just smiled at us. It seemed to set the tone for her life and our life with her. I think about those moments often. Even though I would give her other nicknames like Sug, Cutie, and Silly Sally, in my heart she would always be my sweet Sally.

Less than six months earlier, on July 26, 1984, Anna Grace Jordan was born to Jo's sister, Anne, and her husband, Dick. Seemingly from the moment Sally arrived, she and Grace were together. Even though they attended different schools and had different friends, they lived their lives not just as cousins but as kindred spirits. In each other, they found friendship, laughter, confidence, and peace. In our collection of family photos, we have almost as many photos of the two of them together as we do of Sally alone.

During Sally's first visit with her pediatrician, we learned that her feet were turned in severely. Without taking significant measures, she would have difficulty walking properly.

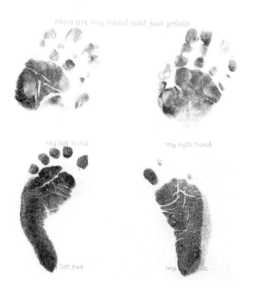

We met with one of the area's top orthopedists, and he told us Sally would need plaster casts on her legs and feet followed by baby shoes that would be attached to metal braces to hold her toes pointing outward for at least a year. It was an extreme but necessary step that needed to be taken while she was young and her bones were still forming. There was no promise Sally's feet would be perfectly straight when the braces came off, but he was confident she would see a significant improvement and be able to walk normally. That was all we needed to hear.

After the plaster casts were removed from Sally's little legs, she wore the tiny white shoes with the toes turned out and a brace attached to the bottom of the shoes for nearly a year. If they bothered her, it never showed. Nothing, it seemed, slowed Sally down. One of my fondest memories was watching her learn to crawl while she dragged the braces behind her. I could even grab her by the braces and hold her upside down while she giggled uncontrollably.

After more than a year, we were allowed to take the braces off Sally's legs as she learned to walk. The casts and braces achieved the goal of straightening Sally's feet, but no one realized the unintended consequences of the treatment, which would hinder Sally's ability to play sports when she got older.

Sally was a "lifer" at Charlotte Country Day, starting with junior kindergarten through her graduation from high school. It was a happy place for Sally, but she had a way of making every place happy. She never lacked for friends who were drawn to her warm smile, her giggle, and her perpetually positive outlook on life. Her glass always seemed to overflow.

She usually didn't let many things annoy her, but once in a while life intruded. One of the few times happened when our family went to Disney World. Sally was five and Reynolds six. Graham would not arrive for another two years. After standing in line for more than an hour to ride Space Mountain, the attendant informed us that Sally was too small to ride. An hour of anticipation, not to mention the rare commodity of youthful patience, was destroyed.

Sally didn't take the news well. She fell to the floor, screaming and crying the way five-year-olds sometimes do. It was a rare but classic meltdown that seemed to have no end. Eventually Jo picked up Sally and carried her away as she continued to kick and scream.

On the other end of the spectrum of emotions was her uncontrollable joy at the birth of her baby brother. On January 21, 1991, God blessed us with our third child, Walter Graham. Sally and Reynolds were beside themselves and took turns holding him at the hospital and for months to come. This set the tone of the special bond that developed between them. I gave him the affectionate nickname of "Little Man."

Sally's priorities as a child were her family first, her friends second, and her passion for music third. Sally loved music and was a beautiful singer, earning a spot in the Honors Choir at Country Day in middle and upper school. Sally's voice was amazing, especially because neither Jo nor I are singers. Jo has a nice voice, but I couldn't carry a tune in a bucket.

Sally and Grace loved to lead us in our blessing when we gathered as a family, singing the version of the "Oh, The Lord Has Been Good to Me" sung to the tune of Johnny Appleseed. It's a family tradition we carry forward to this day, with both girls in mind every time we sing it, sometimes with great emotion as we remember them leading us as little girls.

Though the singing gene escaped me, I love music, and Sally and I liked to listen to music together. That can be a tricky thing for a parent and child, because musical tastes vary from generation to generation. I was fortunate enough to grow up listening to '60s music, one of the greatest musical eras ever, and I wondered—I even worried—what kind of music my children would be drawn to. When I allowed myself to listen to rap as its popularity increased, I hoped that wouldn't be what my children listened to, because the lyrics of some songs were too harsh and vulgar for my taste. I understand that children will pick their own music, but as a dad I hoped they would share my taste in music.

Driving the kids to school each day, I had control of the radio. Typically, I would put it on a '60s station or one that played more contemporary artists, such as Hootie and the Blowfish or Bruce Hornsby. If I wanted pure rock music and a dose of humor, I'd keep the radio on John Boy and Billy's morning show in Charlotte. On the way to school one morning, Reynolds asked if I'd change the station to Kat Country with Paul Schadt. I was shocked. My only exposure to country music was a few songs I'd heard through the years. It was practically foreign to me, and I couldn't imagine my kids being interested in country music. It's just more evidence of how parenting is full of surprises. I asked Sally what she wanted to listen to.

"Dad," she said, "we like your music but we really like country. We listen to it with Mom when she picks us up."

I hadn't seen this coming. As it turned out, someone who worked for us and occasionally picked up the kids had planted the country music seed with them. My kids, in turn, planted that seed in me. The more I listened, the more I found songs that reminded me of the music I had grown up with … but now with a *twank* in the New Country genre. Had it not been for the kids, I might never have realized what I was missing. One of the amazing things I discovered as time progressed was that this genre became the choice of many of her classmates. Rather than being on the outside looking in, Sally was in the mainstream and no doubt converting many like myself to the New Country. We ended up taking many of her friends to concerts and finding others there when we arrived.

Jo and me, Randy and Dianne Dorton, Sally and
Theresa Muzillo backstage at a Brooks and Dunn
concert with their stage manager

Over the years, Jo and I went to country concerts regularly, often with our children, and most often with Sally. We went with her to see Tim McGraw, Faith Hill, George Strait, Kenny Chesney, Brooks and Dunn, Toby Keith, Shania Twain, Martina McBride, and others. For several years, Jo and Sally, along with Anne, Grace, and Katie, Anne's oldest daughter, would drive to Nashville for a week for the annual series of country concerts that comprised Fan Fair. It was strictly a girls' trip. The closest I got to the events was listening to the stories and laughs about whose concerts they had seen, whose autographs they had gotten, and what they had done.

Sally with Chely Wright at Fan Fair

Sally and I also had a shared passion for photography, the ever-changing world of technology, BMW cars, and Tar Heel basketball. She was a full-fledged member of the ABD club (Anybody but Duke!). We had season tickets to the Dean Dome. In the 2004 home game for Carolina against Duke, Carolina lost in overtime during Roy Williams' first year. Sally came over from Peace to go to it and stayed with us that night at the local hotel.

Sally loved BMW cars, and when she got her driver's license she took over our late model black 3 Series convertible. As the frequency of carjackings began to escalate around Charlotte, I became worried about her safety. I offered to buy her a new hardtop BMW if she would part with the convertible. She eagerly agreed. She picked a shade of blue close to Carolina blue, given her love for Carolina basketball.

Although we picked it up immediately following a knee surgery, Sally was determined to drive it home herself. I can still see the smile on her face as she was handed the keys to her new car.

Sally loved taking photographs, particularly of sunsets, and her favorite was of a sunset when she was in Aruba on her senior trip. I keep that photo on the screen of my iPhone, iPad, and my computers as a reminder of Sally and the things she loved.

Sports and outdoor activities were also a big part of Sally's life. When she was young, she played T-ball and softball and seemingly anything else she could find that involved a game and friends or family. Sally simply liked being a part of things that involved others. It even carried as far as going hunting and fishing with her brothers and cousins. She never wanted to be left out.

It didn't matter to Sally whether she was the best at what she did. Being a part of something and sharing the experience with others was what mattered to Sally. I would have been thrilled had Sally developed a passion for playing golf, but that never happened. She would go with us sometimes when we played, but the game never fully captured her. I think the drawback may have been that it was not a team-oriented sport and her friends never developed an interest.

In middle school, Sally wanted to play field hockey and softball, but it turned out that the year she'd spent wearing casts and braces to straighten her feet had created knee problems no one could have foreseen. The corrective devices Sally wore prevented her knees from developing properly.

We found this out the hard way. At the grocery store when Sally was 12, I sent her to another aisle to pick up something. Suddenly, I heard a child screaming and immediately knew it was Sally. When I found her, she was sprawled on the floor and said, "Oh Daddy, my knee hurts." I could see that the kneecap on her right leg had slipped out of place and was on the side of her leg. The sight shocked me. Sally was in pain and I didn't know what to do. Not sure how to help, I asked her if she could stand. When she started to get up, her kneecap popped back into place and the pain instantly disappeared. However, I was immediately concerned that something wasn't right.

Unfortunately, the knee problem occurred again, and we took her to see a highly respected orthopedic surgeon. He told us that the sockets in both of Sally's legs, where the kneecap is supposed to fit, had not properly formed, most likely due to the corrective measures used to straighten her feet. That meant there was a strong likelihood that this would happen again in both legs. Surgery, he said, was an option, but he didn't recommend it at the time. If Sally wanted to continue playing sports, she could as long as she understood the risks.

Sally didn't consider quitting, at least not initially. But when her kneecaps continued to pop out during practice and games, it became difficult for her to keep going and for coaches to put her in to play. Reluctantly, and with great disappointment, Sally came to the realization that she couldn't continue to play competitive sports. That didn't mean abandoning sports, however. She wanted to be around the games and her friends, so she decided to become a team trainer. She spoke with the father of one player, who also was an orthopedic surgeon, and asked if there was anything he could do to fix her knees. He also advised her that surgery would be a difficult path but possible. Sally was determined to play sports again and was prepared to endure surgery on both knees prior to her senior year at Country Day.

During the fall of her 11th grade year, Sally had surgery on her right knee. Unfortunately, the surgery did not achieve the results she or her doctor hoped for, and Sally had additional surgery the following summer on the same knee. Given this, Sally's hope of possibly playing a sport her senior year was never realized.

As a father, boys are a challenge. Not necessarily your own boys, but the boys who are attracted to your daughter and the boys to whom she is attracted. In Sally's case, there were two. Her first crush was on Bill Cummings when they were in middle school. Bill was the son of close friends Steve and Karen Cummings, whose youngest son, Lee, remains one of our son Graham's closest friends.

When Sally was in 11th grade, she met her second love, Graeme Keith. They met when Graeme came along with his father, Greg, to pick up his son Cody, another of Graham's friends.

I would learn later that when the Keiths were leaving our house that day, Graeme—who attended a different school than Sally—asked his father to help him find a way to ask Sally out. Shortly thereafter they began dating and their relationship remained close until Sally's accident. We expected Sally and Graeme, who both maintained a deep Christian faith, to eventually marry.

Sally and Bill in middle school

Sally and Graeme at her Junior/Senior Prom

In a too short life filled with memorable moments, the defining one in Sally's life happened during the summer after her eighth grade year. She was invited by her friend Theresa Muzillo to join her at a weeklong summer camp, Camp Courtney, in the mountains. The camp was put on by Theresa's church, Grace Covenant, and Sally decided to go.

When I drove her to meet Theresa on the Saturday morning when they left for camp, Sally was apprehensive about the trip. She looked forward to the time she would spend with Theresa but she wasn't sure what else she was getting herself into at a Christian camp. We went to church regularly as a family, but finding faith is a personal journey that requires you to find your own way to a belief in God and our salvation through the resurrection of his Son, Jesus Christ.

I walked her to the bus, gave her a hug, and told her to enjoy the week. We would look forward to hearing about it when she returned. This was before cell phones were a part of everyone's life, and there was no communication with the children while they were at camp. The following Friday, I was waiting for Sally when the bus returned to Grace Covenant. I sat in the car watching for Sally to get off the bus, and I was beginning to wonder where she was when she finally stepped off. I was struck by her appearance. There was a visible calm and an aura about her that had not been there when she left. I knew she was at a different place than where she had been when she left a week earlier. It was obviously a good place. There was a peace and happiness about Sally as she walked to the car.

The memory of seeing her come off that bus, a changed person from the one I'd put on it a week earlier, has remained with me. Every parent's hope is that their child will find something positive to build their life around, and she found Christ that week. How this came to pass at the camp she never shared. However, this would define the rest of her life, and I am grateful to those who helped her find Him.

Her priorities changed after Camp Courtney. From then until her death, Sally's faith came first, her family second, and her friends third. Music remained a passion, but her energy and life were directed toward her faith. Following this defining point, Sally became a faithful member of Grace Covenant Church. She rarely missed a service or Sunday School class and became active in youth ministry. She also sang in the youth choir and briefly in the adult choir. On occasion, she was asked to sing solo. Given her new Christian faith, her music interest expanded and broadened to now include Contemporary Christian.

We also learned a couple of years after the accident that the Saturday night she came home at three, Sally sat with friend Tyler Blackmon from church, who was disillusioned about life and had begun drinking and smoking pot. She implored and prayed with him to gain strength from his faith, to believe in himself and change his life. When he learned of the girls' accident the following weekend, he was devastated. He then made the decision to change his life and credited Sally in a story the *Charlotte Observer* ran. The

article highlighted a video he'd produced and edited that focused on the dangers of teen drinking. He spoke in the article about how Sally told him, "God will always love you. So it doesn't matter what others think. You don't need to drink." That was Sally.

Also, about a year after the accident, I took a call from a Chicago phone number. On the other end was a young man who had known Sally from a bike trip she did after her ninth grade year. They had traveled across New England with a company named Overland that puts together summer camps and unique trips for teenagers.

We knew she had made a tremendous impression on the counselors during the trip, who shared how well-liked Sally was by everyone on the trip. They told us how she'd overcome trouble with her knees and had also suffered a breathing attack but would not quit. The young man who called was a fellow rider and asked if what he'd heard about Sally from another friend was true. I told him that heartbreakingly it was indeed true, that she'd lost her life in a car accident. He was devastated and became very emotional. He said he had talked to Sally a number of times while on the trip and had stayed in touch with her for a while afterwards. While not sharing what may have been troubling on their trip, he told me her influence caused him to change his life for the better. He also told me she was the most liked person on their trip and everyone loved her. I thanked him for calling and sharing this. That was Sally.

When it came time for Sally to decide on college, she had her heart set on attending Belmont in Nashville. She wanted to study music, and Belmont was an ideal place for her. To be accepted to Belmont, Sally had to audition for a panel. It was a big step, both exciting and intimidating.

Sally and Jo flew to Nashville, hopeful she would impress the panel enough to get admitted to Belmont. Sally's plan was to sing "Ave Maria," and she practiced intensely to be ready for her audition. But as she and Jo waited for Sally's turn before the panel, they heard other applicants singing and were awed by what they heard. When Jo asked Sally if she felt good about continuing, Sally said, "Mom, I don't, and I believe it's best if I withdraw my application." It was a disappointing decision, but Sally felt like it was the right decision for her.

There are times in our lives when reality intrudes on our dreams. It happened to me with football at Minnesota when I realized, looking around the locker room, that I had peaked in high school. Listening to others sing at Belmont, Sally realized she had already reached the high point in her singing career.

Shortly thereafter, Sally and her friend at Country Day, Nina Schulte, were offered partial academic scholarships to Peace College in Raleigh and they quickly accepted.

In January, following her fall semester, when she had done well academically, Sally told us she really wasn't happy at Peace and wanted to transfer to Carolina. I told her Carolina didn't accept sophomore transfers and suggested she first transfer to UNCC for a year and then transfer to Chapel Hill as a junior. She would also be closer to home, a personal wish of mine. She loved the idea and submitted an application shortly thereafter. We received her letter of acceptance the week following the accident.

8

The Days
That Followed

~

April 11, 2004. Easter Sunday

It was a day Sally always looked forward to. As Easter approached, we had been told that the girls were going to be mentioned during the sermon at Christ Church, Grace Covenant, and the annual sunrise Easter service held at Machpelah Church.

Jo wanted to attend all three. I wasn't sure, especially going back to Machpelah and Grace Covenant, but it was important to me to support Jo. Because it was Easter, all three churches offered multiple services at different times, allowing us to visit each of them. We began with a sunrise service at Machpelah, followed by a mid-morning service at Grace, and the late morning service at Christ Church.

Arriving at Machpelah, I could not help but first look toward the cemetery at our family plot that now included the girls' ashes. It was the first time I'd been back since Tuesday evening when we'd gathered there with family and friends, and it was too much. I wanted to support Jo and hear the minister's message, but I didn't want to be here. I reached as deep as I could within myself for strength, and with Jo, Reynolds, Graham, Grace's family, and many of our friends, made my way into the church. I knew they were all suffering and struggling with their own emotions and heartbreak. I felt that I needed to be there for them.

As with the girls' memorial service, I focused on a spot on the wall to keep my eyes from focusing on others or on the minister. I remember hearing her mention the girls but did not focus on exactly what she said. After the service, we decided to visit the cemetery. I did not want to go but again felt I needed to be there. As we stood looking at the freshly turned earth and the temporary markers and wilting flowers, my heart ached, thinking of my sweet Sally and Grace. The grief was overwhelming. I held on, but in my mind I could not help but wonder what this would look like once more time had passed and the expired flowers were removed. I suspected few would remember.

Both girls loved flowers, particularly sunflowers. I knew I didn't want their final resting place marked by wilted or dead flowers. I couldn't allow this. Several weeks later, I began taking sunflowers and roses there every week, which I continued to do for many years. Even now, most weeks, I still bring them flowers. Each time I place them, the emotions come rushing back, but I can't bear to think of flowers not being there for them.

We went home after the sunrise service and got something to eat before heading quickly to Grace Covenant Church. I took the route that avoided driving by the accident scene. At Grace, all I could think about was Sally. I have no recollection of the service; however, as I sat there, I knew it was a place to which I would not be able to return for some time. Grace Covenant Church meant so much to Sally that I could not separate her life from that church. It was too much for me to bear, and for many years I was not able to return there.

I also have little memory of our final service at Christ Church other than the recollection of the many people at each service who came up to us to express their sorrow and grief at our loss and to express how touched they were that we made the effort to come. Yet, while my own emotions were in shambles, I still couldn't find the tears that went with them.

Following the Easter services, Greg told us the officers investigating the accident wanted to meet with us at our house to discuss their findings the next day. Most of what we knew was limited to what we had learned the two days following the accident. We didn't want to react to the rumors that had reached us—we wanted to know what had happened. Anne and Dick, along with their children, joined us to meet with the officers.

On Monday, three officers came to our home. What they told us shook everyone. Based on their investigation, Shimp had gone to a bar in Cornelius to celebrate with friends his graduation from the NASCAR Technical Institute in Mooresville. Over the course of an hour-and-a-half, based on what they had been able to piece together, he was served six beers and three shooters. Hearing this, all kinds of emotions and thoughts ran through me. More and more, a feeling of anger developed. Beyond Shimp's own role in taking Sally and Grace from us, I found fault in those who were with him that night. Beyond the thought of how anyone could drink this much and still stand, it was more overwhelming to think that others could allow a friend or companion to get behind the wheel of a car knowing how much alcohol they had consumed. Even if they didn't care what happened to him, how could they not think of others he would put at risk by driving under the influence? Worse still, how could the bartender and those who served him continue to give him more to drink and why hadn't they prevented him from driving? Why hadn't they called a taxi or called the police?

We learned that Shimp was indeed going to be charged with two counts of second-degree murder and his bond was set at nearly one million dollars, ensuring that he would remain in custody until his trial. While I had no idea when, I trusted that the criminal justice system would deal with him and the horrible decisions he'd made that night.

I knew, however, that it would be difficult for me to ever forgive him. I still could not understand why, having had as much to drink as Shimp had, he would drive 90 miles an hour. I understand alcohol alters our decision-making, but it didn't help me make peace with the reality. Behind the wheel after having that much to drink, Shimp was a loaded gun waiting to be fired.

And it wasn't just Shimp who was at fault. I also felt the bar was guilty for serving someone that much and then letting him walk out the door. The bar had actually loaded his gun for him. As I processed this, I resolved to hold them accountable by any means available to us and planned to discuss this with Jo, Anne, and Dick. As for Shimp's friends, they were going to have to live with themselves, knowing they had allowed their friend to drive away and, in addition to destroying his own life, take the lives of two precious girls and seriously injure another.

Following our meeting, I told Jo, Anne, and Dick that beyond our need for legal representation for Shimp's trial, based on what we'd just learned, I also wanted to discuss with an attorney whether the bar broke any laws and could be charged in a criminal court or sued in civil court. We agreed it would be best to do so together rather than for each family to obtain their own attorney.

As I continued to process what we'd just heard, the heartbreak grew more intense. Beyond my own sense of guilt, it was clear that many others had had the chance to do something and didn't. The knife of pain and heartbreak, with all its barbs, continued to dig deeper into me with no sense of the pain ceasing.

The following day we were given the personal items Sally had with her that night. Among the items was a Christian cross we'd given her. It was one of her most precious possessions, and she wore it every day. Jo wears it now. Also, Sally had purchased a silver bracelet with the Christian fish as its hook. I now wear that constantly. We decided later to have replicas of the bracelet made to give to others who loved her and to those who helped us in special ways in our efforts to honor her memory as time went on.

We were also given her phone. Seeing it brought back the heartbreaking memories of our desperate pleas that night for her to answer. That was the hardest. It symbolized so much I didn't want to remember. What we didn't find was the watch we'd given her. We didn't know if it was in the car and asked Greg if he could contact the wrecker service to see if it might be there. It wasn't.

Jo later received a call from a friend of Sally's who had gone to the accident scene the day following the accident. She found Sally's watch next to the gutter across the street from the location of the accident. When Jo told me, I couldn't allow myself to think of the implications that watch represented. I didn't think the knife could dig any deeper, but it did.

While Peace College had been devastated by the loss of a student and more than understanding about our need for time, they finally told us to come and clean out her dorm room. Again, it was a place where I couldn't go. However, there was no way to avoid the need to go and retrieve Sally's belongings from her room.

In addition to cleaning out her room at Peace, we also needed to get Sally's car from the boys' apartment. I didn't want to face any of these tasks, but Jo, with her amazing strength, made plans for us to take care of things. Dianne Dorton offered to go with us to Peace and would drive Sally's car back to their home until we were ready for it.

Knowing we only wanted to make one trip to Raleigh, we took two cars in order to pack everything. I rode alone, while Jo and Dianne rode together in the other car. The sense of despair I felt as I drove and then pulled into the same parking lot where we'd come the previous August to move Sally into her dorm room was overwhelming. I remembered how excited Sally had been about beginning college and what lay ahead. Her life away from home was about to bloom. Now we were returning to her room to remove her things at the end of her life.

I was afraid of how I would react. I also worried about how I'd handle myself if any of her classmates approached us and was concerned about what they might say. Jo continued to demonstrate amazing strength and, with Dianne, headed straight to her room. Tentatively, I followed behind.

We had learned earlier in the week that Sally's friend and roommate, Nina Schulte, from Country Day, had withdrawn from school. Nina was devastated and could not cope with remaining there. She eventually transferred to another school. Her parents had already been there to retrieve her things. Everything that remained in the room had belonged to Sally.

Walking into Sally's dorm room took my breath away, as I know it did for Jo and Dianne as well. The door was covered with cards, as was the floor in front of it. In the middle of the doorway was a small flowering plant that appeared to be dead. I couldn't bring myself to read the cards. Jo and Dianne began collecting the cards along with the plant. I have little recollection of what happened after we walked into Sally's room or what we found there. Jo gave me assignments and I handled them as quickly as I could. I didn't want to linger there. I wanted to be done and gone. I remember several students passing by but none spoke to us. I'm sure they didn't know what to say. As quickly as we could, we loaded the cars and headed home.

The plant we found at Sally's door now flourishes at Jo's mother's home. We call it Sally's plant. Her mother nursed it back to health and has taken shoots to make other plants that she has given to others. The first of many ways Sally's enduring spirit lives on.

The Crown of Thrones plant
left at Sally's dorm door

When we pulled in to get Sally's car and I saw the blue BMW she loved so much parked where she had left it, the pain stabbed me once more. Nothing, it seemed, could numb the hurt and sorrow. Dianne drove Sally's car to her home, and it stayed there for months before it would move again.

Several days later, Jo remembered that Sally had recorded a song on a CD with someone from Grace Covenant. This revelation sent us scouring through her CD collection to see if we could find it. We eventually found it in the CD folder she carried with her. In her beautiful handwriting was "In the Secret" by Sally Clark. Jo remembered it was a contemporary Christian song that had been sung a few years earlier by the group of the same genre, MercyMe, and written by Andy Park. Finding Sally's recording of it brought on all kinds of emotions. I was relieved that we found it but unsure how I would handle listening to her sweet voice. With much apprehension, we put it in a CD player and hit play. It started with someone playing a guitar, and then Sally began to sing.

"In the secret, in the quiet place
In the stillness, You are there.
In the secret, in the quiet hour I wait,
Only for You, 'cause I want to know You more ..."

Jo and I just sat and stared at each other, unsure how to react. As the song finished, I looked at the LCD display on the front of the player. Sally had labeled the CD with just this one song "On the Road to Nashville." I imagined she decided on the title hoping to attend Nashville's Belmont University, or maybe to one day sing or work in the music industry there. I wanted to cry but still couldn't. Sally now knew Him more.

To be certain we'd never lose it, I imported it into my iTunes library. It would be years before I could listen to it again. It was too hard.

9

Where Do We Go From Here?

～

As the devastation of life without Sally continued to take hold and our friends gradually backed away to return to their own lives, Jo and I realized we were going to have to find our way on our own. While we knew our friends would continue to be there if we needed them, this was the beginning of our personal walk as grieving parents. But how we would do it, neither of us had a clue. We heard that more than half the couples who lose a child end up unable to cope with it and divorce. We pledged we would do everything possible to keep this from happening with us. Jo suggested we go for help and meet with a grief counselor. I reluctantly agreed.

We were able to quickly get an appointment with Palmer Trice of the Barnabas Center. As our session began, Palmer asked us what we hoped to get from our meeting. Without hesitation, Jo told him she didn't want to end up divorced like so many others. Palmer looked startled to hear this but agreed the statistics were not in our favor. He said it would take a lot of understanding and give and take by both of us. We would need to give each other our own time and space, as people rarely deal with such a loss in the same way. He also said we would grieve together but would need to allow each other to grieve apart.

Of all we discussed, this advice so close in time to the accident was by far the most critical. More than anything, it helped us respect each other and how we would each choose to process losing Sally. It probably saved us from becoming another statistic.

As we drove home, Jo told me she saw her bible study groups as her personal place of comfort and support and encouraged me to think of where I might find the same. I had no idea what I was going to do. I had wonderful friends, but I knew I would not go to them for support. While knowing they would be there if I asked, my heart and mind were in total turmoil with no sense of where to go or what to do.

Still, I had to get away, if for no other reason than to process all that was being thrown at us. Beyond the devastation of losing Sally, we had to eventually endure Shimp's trial, which would cause even more pain and heartbreak. I also knew I was determined to go after the bar that had served him and let him drive away. I needed time to think about all of this and to get away to be alone with my thoughts.

Earlier in the year I had taken a couple of lessons from Gale Peterson at Sea Island. She had suggested Jo and I come down for a golf school they were offering in late April. The dates didn't fit Jo's schedule but she suggested I go anyway. As the date grew closer I wasn't sure whether to go, but I began to think of it as the opportunity for some time on my own.

However, going to Sea Island posed enormous emotional risks. For many years we'd taken our family there for summer vacation. We had just been there the previous summer and Grace had come with us. It was one of our more memorable trips, and I'd taken some great pictures of Jo and the girls on the dock fishing with Graham, his cousin Dan Paustian, and friend Phillip Hamilton.

Susan Brown, who had hardly left our side since our call for help, along with several others, tried to discourage me from going, worried about me being alone. After much thought, I decided to go. I didn't know what was in store for me but felt it offered the best chance to cope on my own with the enormity of our loss. I couldn't ignore the growing sense of urgency to get away. My mind was in turmoil. Before I left, Jo gave me a journal to write in if I felt compelled. A friend of hers who had lost a son suggested that journaling could help both of us. I didn't think it was something I would do, but I brought it with me just in case.

On the way there, I found myself talking out loud to Sally. I told her I loved and missed her and asked that she forgive me for not telling her to stay at the apartment. What happened, I told her, was all my fault. Again, I wanted to cry but still couldn't.

As I drove along Interstate 26 between Columbia and Interstate 95, near the exit where our family always stopped for gas and a bathroom break on our way to Sea Island, a bright light suddenly began to shine through my windshield. It was radiant and unlike anything I'd ever seen. I was stunned and could not comprehend its source. I began to slow down, but the light remained on my windshield until it finally disappeared. I didn't know how long it had lasted, but it left me shaken. I pulled into a rest stop just down the highway to regroup.

Was this Sally or God, or both, communicating with me to let me know she is okay and not to blame myself? I wondered. I drove the rest of the way trying to make sense of what had occurred. Today, given so many other things that have shown me God and Sally's hands at work, I believe they were letting me know not to blame myself for what had happened.

As I drove across the causeway to Sea Island, the dock where Sally and Grace had been last summer came into view. My heart went to my throat. I knew immediately I'd made a mistake to come. The memories were too fresh and too painful to be back so soon.

While Gale and the others conducting the school tried to help and offer comfort, I could not focus and left a day earlier than planned. However, during the two nights I was there, I wrote letters to Sally in the book Jo had given me.

Friday, April 23, 2004
My Sweet Sally:

It has now been almost three weeks since you went home to the Lord. Rarely a moment goes by that I am not thinking of you. You were a bright light in a dark world and brought great joy and happiness to your mother and me. It remains difficult for me to accept you are not here with us. I have visions of your warm sweet smile vivid in my mind and yearn to see you in front of me. You brought me much happiness and no pain except for this. When I reflect on your short wonderful life here, I look at a rare human being that tried very hard to please those around you and sought little in return. I have vivid memories of the time we went to dinner with you, and your mother and I quarreled. You would get extremely upset with us and rightfully so. It is now my hope and commitment that for the remaining years I have on this earth, I refuse to engage in that behavior in honor of your memory.

Right now, as I hope you and the Lord look down on me, I am at Sea Island in a golf school, which I'm sure doesn't surprise you. I am struggling with frequent memories of the wonderful times we had here. The picture from last year of you and Grace on the dock with the crab is etched in my mind, but more so is the picture of you trying to bait your hook. It is such a telling picture of you and the fun you had doing something you probably didn't want to do. The other thing I am struggling with since you left us for the Lord is what to do about the new BMW I ordered that we talked about and shared. We are going to keep your car for sure, because I cannot bear the thought of parting with it. It was so much a part of you and something you really loved. How we choose to drive it I'm not sure, but I hope you give us guidance from Heaven. Please help me to decide on the other car.

I read your journal today or parts of it for the first time. Sug, I continue to be in awe of your perspective on the world and your innocent but genuine love of your Lord and where you chose to seek help. It speaks volumes about the person you were. I only wish at your age, and now, I was half the person you were in your earthly form. I could not be prouder.

Well, I have still much to say but need to call your mom now. I will continue the first chance I get.

With as much love as I can muster,
Your admiring Dad

Saturday, April 24, 2004
My Sweet Sally:

Another day has passed since you went home to the Lord, and I'm still struggling with the realization I will never see you again on this earth. I realize it even more now than before. You provided me with immense joy and happiness. I think of the things we shared. Our love of Carolina basketball, the Panthers, and for the most part, sports in general. Also, cars and country music.

It is difficult for me to comprehend that I don't have you to talk with about these. However, I am comforted by the thought you are with the Lord and that I can connect with you through him. While I cannot explain or totally understand the experience I had on Thursday on my drive here to Sea Island, I know the vision I had was a sign from you or the Lord that you are near. I can only hope that someday I will understand or at least gain some sense of what I felt and saw. I will leave it in the Lord's hands to help with this.

While I know this is random, I feel it is necessary to mention the outpouring of love and support your mother, brothers, and I have received due to your passing. It speaks volumes about how people feel about this and the many lives you touched during your short stay here.

I am deeply grateful the Lord shared you with us.

I realize I am rambling so I probably need to say goodnight and I love you as much love as a dad can muster.

I love you,

Dad

I returned home in a far worse place than when I left. The memories of Sally and Grace on the dock the previous summer and our numerous family vacations there were too much. I also canceled the order for the BMW SUV I'd ordered to replace our Suburban when I got home, because I could not think of getting it without her. I called Greg Hayes at Hendrick BMW, whom I'd worked with for many years. He had helped Sally and me order her car and this one. Greg completely understood.

10

The Roll of Toilet Paper

I continued to feel completely lost. I didn't know where to go or how to grieve on my own as Palmer Trice had suggested. My world continued to implode. On May 1, Dianne planned a surprise 50th birthday party for Randy, at Red Rocks Restaurant in Birkdale Village, directly across from where the accident had happened. I wanted to attend the party but told Dianne not to expect us. There were still flowers at the accident scene, and I wasn't prepared to go back there so soon.

The day before the party, Dianne called to tell us she had found a route that would get us to the restaurant without going past the accident site. We could wind through a neighborhood and avoid what I wanted to avoid. We went but I couldn't enjoy the celebration. I couldn't shake my sadness. It would take years for us to reengage in social gatherings even on a small level. We began to avoid parties. Heartbreak will do that to a person.

As we were leaving the party, Jimmie Johnson and his soon-to-be wife, Chandra Janway (Chani to her friends), spoke to us, expressing their sorrow over what had happened. Jo had met them at a race in Phoenix the previous year, but I had not met them before. They were clearly emotional as they spoke, and we were touched by their willingness to share their feelings with us.

I was struck by how genuine Jimmie and Chani were. They were approachable, and I sensed the sincerity of their words. Given Jimmie's superstardom in auto racing, they could have been distant. Instead, they were the opposite, and we felt tremendous gratitude for their genuine and heartfelt caring.

Over time, we've gotten to know them better, and our initial impressions have been reinforced. They are classy, humble, and unfazed by their celebrity status. Beyond being, in my opinion, the greatest NASCAR driver ever, Jimmie is a great ambassador for the sport. As a couple, they put a wonderful face on the racing scene.

The following week the Wachovia Championship began at Quail Hollow, a PGA Tour event sponsored by the Charlotte-based bank. This was the second year it was held at Quail Hollow. After much thought, I decided to go to the Wednesday Pro-Am by myself. Walking by the golf shop, I passed Rich Davies, a good friend who had just finished playing in the event. I had not spoken to Rich since Sally's accident, and he approached me with tears in his eyes, expressing his sorrow over what had happened.

Rich put his hands on my shoulders and shared a story about an event that had happened to him while he was attending grade school in his native South Africa. He told me about a teacher who had walked into the classroom one day and unexpectedly unrolled a roll of toilet paper down a center aisle between the students. The teacher then asked the students what the toilet paper represented. Rich said he and classmates snickered at seeing toilet paper on the classroom floor, but no one had an answer for the teacher.

The length of the toilet paper, the teacher said, represented the history of humanity on earth. While holding his index finger and thumb a fraction of an inch apart, he told the students that the tiny distance represented the amount of time their lives accounted for in that history. Their obligation was to make a difference while they were here.

Rich said that whether we live to be a 100 or 19, the difference in the timeline of humanity is miniscule. While Rich did not know Sally, he told me he had heard so much about her from others. It was apparent that although she was only here for 19 years, she'd made a difference in her time, and it was important for me to know that.

With his words and wisdom, for the first time since April 4, I found a small foothold to stop my freefall. I also felt for the first time a small sense of consolation about losing Sally. Knowing how fragile life is and that there are no guarantees we will die before our children—as every parent prays will happen—this story gave me a perspective that I would not have otherwise considered. Most significant of all, it came when I desperately needed something to pull me from my gathering depression. Beyond the devastation of losing my only daughter, I understood that Sally was a special human being. Hearing someone relate that others perceived her the same way was both enormous and meaningful to me.

11

A Safe Harbor

After the tournament concluded and members were allowed back at the club, I began going there almost daily searching for personal peace and a place to grieve on my own, as Jo and I had decided earlier we both needed. There seemed to be no other place that could offer me what I felt I could find there. Quail Hollow is where I played most of my golf and where I loved to practice. Losing myself in the strange joy of hitting golf balls on the range gave me private space. It was a place where I could go and be by myself as I practiced my swing. I preferred to go to the back of the practice range where I could be alone, hitting ball after ball and coping with my emotions. I had little desire to play and began to decline invitations from friends who asked me to join them. There was just something about playing and engaging with others I wanted to avoid if at all possible.

On occasion, Eric Williamson, one of the assistants at the time, would stop by while I practiced to just say hello and offer to help me. I began taking him up on it, and beyond the discussion about my swing, I would share with him some of the thoughts running through my head about losing Sally. More than the golf, Eric was wonderful in just allowing me to release some of what had built up inside. I needed someone to talk to but knew I wasn't going to seek professional help. Eric's help, support, and understanding were exactly what I needed.

When I was finished practicing, I would find a table off from the main sitting area on the club veranda overlooking the 18th hole and sit there for hours, alone with my thoughts and grief as I looked down at the green. I eventually began to take golf books of golf courses in the British Isles along with me, including Donald Steel's book.

I also took photo albums of my trips there. I had finally made it back in 1986 and many more times over the following years. As I sat and looked at the books and pictures from those trips, a sense of calm would come over me. While the club offered a physical safe harbor, the pictures and books provided a mental safe harbor that momentarily quieted the storm raging in my mind. Looking through them, a flood of memories rushed in—momentous, happy times filled with fun and adventure. What great memories they were!

12

Special Memories For
A Brokenhearted Father

As I had hoped back in 1984, I made it to Scotland to just play golf for the first time in 1986, but it didn't happen the way I thought. After a year-and-a-half of trying unsuccessfully to get a group together from Quail Hollow, I accepted an offer from Barry Ward, the owner of the travel agency I was using, to join another group—with one notation. The group would be entirely composed of members of Duke's athletic booster group, the Iron Dukes. For someone who'd gone to North Carolina, this was something significant to consider. However, I wanted to go so bad I didn't care and told Barry I was ready to go.

I flew out of Charlotte on July 23, 1986, to join the group at Turnberry, where The Open had been played the week before. It was pouring rain when I arrived Sunday afternoon in Glasgow, but I didn't care. I had made it to Scotland to play golf for a week. I was finally going to play links golf.

When I arrived at Turnberry it was still raining. I could see the grandstands in place around the Ailsa course from The Open Championship. It was every bit of a wow moment, as we were set to play it the next morning. Through the rain and clouds, I could also barely make out the Ailsa Craig rock in the distance, an instantly recognizable landmark on Open Championship telecasts from Turnberry.

After settling into my room on the backside of the hotel, I crashed from the long trip before heading downstairs for a welcoming cocktail party in the bar. Walking down the majestic staircase as I reached the main floor, the sun had come out and was sparkling off the sea and the golf course next to it. Oh my! I ordered a lager, settled into a comfortable chair looking west over the course, and thought how lucky I was to be there. Then it got even better. From my left, I could hear the sound of bagpipes approaching the hotel. I could sense the hair on my neck stand up. When I saw the piper, I just sat there taking it all in. It was an exquisite Scottish golf moment, and it set the tone for a memorable week.

When Barry joined me a few minutes later, he told me that he'd informed his group another golfer from Charlotte would be joining them during the trip. Though Barry had been born and raised in England, he understood the dynamic of the Duke-North Carolina rivalry.

The group included some husbands and wives, and when I introduced myself to Randy and Jo Ely, they asked when I had attended Duke. There was no escape. I confessed that I went to Carolina, and they both erupted in laughter, praising my bravery. Randy then told the rest of the group I was a North Carolina alum, and pretty soon they all came over to welcome me.

The group included Duke athletic director Tom Butters and longtime men's golf coach Rod Myers. While my expectations for the golf were understandably high, the time I spent with the group turned out to be the highlight. There were so many tremendous people, and I stayed in touch with several for years following our trip.

Over the next week, we played the Ailsa Course at Turnberry, Royal Troon, Western Gailes, Prestwick, Muirfield, Carnoustie, and the Old and New Courses at St. Andrews. A dream list of links courses! We also played the Kings Course at Gleneagles I had passed on in 1984 while there with Jo. It didn't take long into our golf to realize the shots I typically hit at home, high shots that tended to stop quickly, didn't work on the bouncy links turf. At Prestwick the afternoon of our first day, I caught the wrath of my caddie, who grew tired of seeing me fly shots to the hole only to see them run off the back of the green. He kept saying, "Laddie, you cannot play American golf on a links course. You need to play it where I tell ya!"

Gradually, I adjusted my game and paid close attention to his advice on the club to hit, the line to take, and the spot to place my approach shot to the pin, no matter how ridiculous I thought it seemed. My improved scores reflected my compliance and won his approval.

The next day we played Royal Troon in the morning. However, the weather turned bad as we finished and many in our group decided to skip the afternoon round at Western Gailes. We teed off in a driving rain. It reminded me of the scene from *Caddyshack* when the priest is playing the round of his life and refuses to let a raging thunderstorm stop him. It was dark and gloomy with the wind whipping the rain, but I played what would be my best round of the trip, shooting even-par despite the conditions. As good as that was, and it remains one of my most memorable days on a golf course anywhere, the best, however, was saved for last.

The day before we were to return home, we played our last round over the Kings Course at Gleneagles in a wind that literally bent the flagsticks horizontal. It was an exhausting round and, as much as I had enjoyed the golf and my new friends, I missed Jo, Reynolds, and Sally. I was ready to go home.

We were staying at the hotel I classified as an eyesore in 1984, the Old Course Hotel in St. Andrews. Before dinner, our entire group met in the Road Hole Bar on the top floor for a drink. While there, the sun finally appeared, painting the Old Course in a beautiful light. Reminiscing about the trip with Coach Myers and two men whose names I have regrettably forgotten, and looking at the scene before us, I was spellbound. As we sat and enjoyed the moment, Coach Myers said, "I'm not quite ready to let this end. Anybody interested in playing?"

Without being asked a second time, we jumped to our feet and headed to our room to change out of our coats and ties and put on our golf clothes again. We grabbed our clubs from storage, climbed over the old stone wall behind the hotel, and walked to the second tee of the Old Course. The course was empty. It was all ours for the evening and off we went. There was a magical feel to the moment. The air was electrical. As we played up the 18th hole with the sun slowly setting, I felt like I was walking on air. This was for me golf at its finest and I couldn't wait to get back.

My love affair with Royal Dornoch officially began in 1987, when Rick Reilly wrote a great article for *Sports Illustrated* magazine about spending a week there playing golf. The story focused primarily on his time with caddie Sandy Matheson. Reilly, in his classic style, captured the essence of Royal Dornoch's reputation as the best course no one had ever heard of. He wrote: "Golf Magazine ranks Dornoch as the 12th best course in the world, though anyone who has played it knows that that's low. But what are the people at *Golf* supposed to do, seeing as hardly anyone has ever heard of it? It's like W (the magazine) naming Mrs. Eva Dalrymple of Cedar Rapids, Iowa, as the best dressed, but nobody has ever heard of her. So 12th is as good as she's going to get."

Reilly brilliantly conveyed the allure of Royal Dornoch, particularly its status before the world seemed to discover it. Reilly related a question he asked his caddie over a glass of Maclellan single malt following his first round at Dornoch. The anecdote captured the unique and special humor one can find in Scottish caddies. Reilly wrote: "That night Sandy and I sat there making love to our Maclellan, and I said to Sandy, 'Have you drunk Maclellan all your life?' And Sandy said, 'Not yet!'"

~

In 1988, I came over in late July with 11 other men, mostly from Quail Hollow, to play many of the same courses I'd played in 1986, along with Royal Dornoch and Gullane No. 1. We started our trip at Dornoch. After settling in at the Burghfield House Hotel late in the afternoon, we planned to play 36 holes. As fate would have it, Sandy caddied for our group. While he didn't carry my bag, he was in my foursome both rounds. Everything Rick wrote about him was dead on.

Royal Dornoch starts gently with an easy par-4 followed by a demanding par-3 second, where it quickly becomes obvious how Donald Ross, one of the greatest golf course architects who grew up there, developed his design style. Still, as I walked toward the third tee I wondered if Royal Dornoch was truly as good as advertised and I worried if some of our group would be disappointed in the course.

As I emerged from the gorse-trimmed path that leads to the third tee, my breath was taken away. Royal Dornoch—the body and soul of the course—lay before me in all its ancient majesty. It was big and rolling and magical. It reminded me of how I felt seeing St. Andrews and the R&A clubhouse for the first time four years earlier. This is why we'd come to Royal Dornoch, and I fell under its spell.

After 36 holes of exhilarating golf, the group gathered back at the Burghfield House. When dinner was finished, we moved to the bar where the hotel's proprietor, Euan Currie, held court. He wore a kilt and had the face of a man who has enjoyed his share of single malts. He kept us laughing through the night and escorted us to the hotel's back lawn, where we watched the sun slowly set with a glass of Glenmorangie, the local single malt, in our hands. It had been four years since I'd tasted a single malt back at the Tulchan Lodge, and my appreciation for a good whisky was growing.

In 1990, Jo came with me for the first time to play golf in Scotland with friends Buck and Debbie Wearn. The plan was for Jo and Debbie, after a week of golf, to fly home and Buck and I would fly to Ireland to meet up with six men and play golf in Ireland over the course of another week. With Jo and Debbie, we played Turnberry, Muirfield, Cruden Bay, Nairn, and Royal Dornoch. This marked the beginning of our shared love of links golf and our love affair with Royal Dornoch.

After we saw Jo and Debbie off, Buck and I flew to Belfast. The reality of life in Northern Ireland intruded on us immediately as "The Troubles" were never far away. That's what the locals called the ongoing fighting that had torn their country apart.

After boarding a coach to take us to our hotel, we were stopped by a policeman who boarded our bus with a machine gun slung over his shoulder. He asked our driver our purpose for being there, and he carefully studied each of us as he walked down the aisle. After passing the policeman's inspection and checking into our hotel, we wanted to play golf. We were booked to play Royal Portrush the next morning and Royal County Down a day later, but we decided to squeeze in nine holes at County Down to get us started.

We were met by a lively group of teenaged caddies at County Down, and the good-natured tone was set on the first tee that afternoon. Dick Jonas was given the honor of hitting the first shot of our visit. He hit a pop up that went maybe 50 yards. The caddies burst out laughing, and the one carrying Dick's bag, a young man named Darren, tried to hand his bag to another kid. It was a classic, funny moment, and it wasn't the last one on our trip. Two days later, with Darren caddying for Buck and me, I was the one feeling the sting of his humor.

Playing Royal Portrush the next day was a thrill. There are golf courses and then there are places like Portrush. It deserves its grand reputation. The first hole is fairly soft but from there, it's a solid, man-sized golf course. I was proud of the 89 I shot there.

We returned to Royal County Down the following day. It is one of the truly special courses in the world. It has been ranked among the world's best courses in virtually every ranking, and it belongs there. Anyone who has walked to the edge of the hill in front of the ninth tee and not felt a rush at seeing the iconic Slieve Donard Hotel and the church steeple at the base of the Mourne Mountains is missing the beauty and majesty around them. It touches you.

Darren's Irish humor struck early in our round. On one of our first holes, I managed to find one of the many deep and penal fairway bunkers that give the great links so much of their character. Unlike so many American courses, when you find a bunker at a course like County Down, it's likely to cost you at least one stroke.

After surveying my options in the bunker, I asked Darren for the new 60-degree wedge I had purchased for this trip. With a devilish smile, Darren said, "You'll need a 90 to get your ball out of that lie." Buck nearly fell down from laughing so hard. To this day, he reminds me about Darren's zinger. I again barely broke 90 but felt I had gotten the most from my game. That's the challenge of

County Down, despite shooting a higher score than I had hoped, I felt like I had earned what I shot.

With Portrush and County Down as starters, I thought if the rest of our trip could come close to matching those two courses, I might have to give Ireland the edge over Scotland in terms of my favorite courses. After a night at the Slieve Donard, we headed south to Dublin. But first another adventure awaited us, a true case of dumb and dumber.

Approaching the border between Northern Ireland and Ireland, we arrived at a checkpoint that reminded me of those I'd seen on TV between East and West Germany. A massive hole had been dug to house the checkpoint, which was surrounded by sandbags and machine gun nests occupied by camouflaged British soldiers who weren't smiling. This was serious business for serious men.

Above all of this was a huge sign that read, "ABSOLUTELY NO PHOTOGRAPHY ALLOWED."

That didn't stop Ed Dalrymple, who immediately grabbed his camera and said, "I've got to get a picture of this."

Dumb.

As soon as Ed grabbed his camera, a soldier saw him, pointed him out, and ordered our coach to stop. He boarded our bus and took Ed and his camera into an interrogation room. We weren't sure if we'd ever see Ed again. As we sat there waiting, a couple of guys in our group told me, "Clark, you've got to get this on video."

I discreetly reached for my video camera and edged it into the aisle so I could capture what was happening. If Ed had been dumb, I was dumber. Had I been caught, given what had just happened with Ed, I might have been locked in a jail never to be heard from again. Fortunately, Ed was eventually released with his camera but without the film. We were told to keep moving, and we didn't hesitate to be on our way.

Over the next few days we played Portmarnock, Royal Dublin, Killarney, and Ballybunion. We played our final round at Lahinch. The Lahinch we played in 1990 and the one that exists today are different courses. The greens have been rebuilt to the original design, and several holes, most notably the sixth, have been immensely improved. Lahinch is now worthy of the tremendous accolades it receives, though Royal Portrush and Royal County Down remain in a class of their own.

After playing Lahinch, someone suggested a side trip to the Cliffs of Moher. I'd never heard of them, but I went happily along for the ride. Wow! In 1990, there were no guardrails along the cliffs at the main tourist area, allowing you to walk to the edge if you were brave enough. It's a magnificent place, especially peering over the edge to the waves crashing on the rocks hundreds of feet below. It amazed and scared me that some people actually sat on the edge of these enormous cliffs with their feet dangling over the edge. They were as dumb as the rock on which they were perched.

Looking at the staggering beauty and the enormous drop to the water, someone suggested we hit golf balls into the Atlantic and, of course, we couldn't resist. For about 30 minutes, we fired golf balls off the edge of the cliff and into the ocean. We may not have been much smarter than the people sitting on the cliff's edge, but I had a memory of a lifetime.

In 1995, Jo and I brought our family. This time I wanted to attend The Open Championship, which would again be played over the Old Course. We found a home to rent in a small community named Brewlands, about an hour's drive from St. Andrews. The home was named Wester Brewlands. George H.W. Bush and his family had spent parts of several summers there, and we were fortunate that it fit into our budget. The house was big enough that we invited Jo's parents to join us along with Christopher Jordan, Anne's son, who beyond being his first cousin, was Reynolds' closest friend. This remains our family's most memorable trip, loaded with one special memory after another, many of them at St. Andrews and The Open Championship.

We arrived the Sunday before The Open and used the first couple of days to settle in. We could not have found a better place to stay than Wester Brewlands. Beyond the golf, we took everyone to see Edinburgh Castle and other parts of the city, Scone Palace, where kings of Scotland had been crowned, and Glamis Castle, the ancestral home of the Queen Mother. Additionally, the property around Wester Brewlands was full of creeks and ponds, or as they're called there, burns and lochs, where the children waded and fished. Graham also kept us laughing when he referred to the British currency of Pound Sterling as weights.

On Wednesday, we headed to St. Andrews for the first time, and I did my best to give Reynolds, Sally, and Christopher a short bio on the players they were watching as we made our way around the Old Course. Most notably, they got to see Arnold Palmer as he played his final Open Championship. Seeing Davis Love III on the putting green, I told him his aunt and uncle lived near us in Lincoln County and their son Doug was one of my best friends in high school. Davis came over, spoke, and signed autographs for the kids, who were ecstatic over their brush with one of the game's true stars.

At the practice tee a few minutes later, we found a skinny kid hitting balls with his instructor. It was Tiger Woods, who was just 19 years old. I told everyone in our group to take notice, because he seemed destined to become the game's next great player and they were going to hear a lot about him in the coming years. I was right about Tiger, but it's not always so easy predicting the future.

As Woods was hitting balls, another amateur—Gordon Sherry—was also getting his share of attention. He was expected to follow in the line of Nick Faldo as the next great player from the UK. Though Sherry played well in that Open Championship, he soon faded from the scene.

At St. Andrews again on Saturday of The Open, Sally wasn't feeling well. She'd been fighting a bug of some sort on the trip and, shortly after finding a great spot next to the 16th green and 17th tee, she told me she was going to be sick. I told Jo's father that I might have to drive Sally back to Wester Brewlands, although she insisted on staying. She went looking for a restroom, but before she could find one, she made a mad dash for a cluster of gorse bushes beyond a rock wall. Waiting for her, I felt bad that I'd let her come, knowing she wasn't feeling well. I offered to drive her back, but she refused, saying she felt better and wanted to stay with us at the course. I wasn't sure I fully believed her; however, she was fine the rest of the day and it turned into a memorable afternoon.

Sally, Reynolds, and Christopher at The Open

Several players—I particularly remember Steve Elkington—noticed Sally near the 17th tee and gave her a golf ball, much to the disappointment of Christopher and Reynolds. They didn't stand a chance against a 10-year-old girl with a smile like Sally's. When Tom Watson and Greg Norman came by in the same group, former president George H.W. Bush was following them. As he walked by, Christopher shouted, "Hey, George!" The former president smiled and waved at the kids—memories that still sparkle today.

Jo and I came for the final round, leaving the kids with their grandparents. I had acquired special tickets through the R&A that gave us seats near the 17th green and a parking pass, a great deal for us. We spent most of the chilly afternoon watching from our bleacher seats, which also afforded us a beautiful look up the 18th fairway toward the R&A clubhouse. I couldn't have picked a better spot.

If I made a mistake that day, it was this: I forgot the old adage that it ain't over 'til it's over. After seeing Daly salvage a bogey from the Road Hole bunker at No. 17 and par the 18th to maintain his one-stroke lead over Rocca, I told Jo we should think about leaving soon, depending on what Rocca did on the 17th. A par sent Rocca to 18 needing a birdie to force a playoff, not a huge ask on the short finishing hole.

Rather than remain in our seats, I suggested we walk down and watch the 18th hole from along the fairway so we could get to our car quicker. Rocca seemed in perfect position to make birdie after a big tee shot, but then the unimaginable happened—he chunked his second shot, leaving it in the famous Valley of Sin in front of the 18th green. He'd wasted his chance to tie Daly, so Jo and I headed to our car.

That's when we heard the roar that exploded when Rocca holed his improbable twisting birdie putt that sent him to his knees and into a playoff with Daly. The unimaginable had happened again—and this time we had missed it. We listened to Daly win the playoff on the BBC and thought about all we had seen—and what we had missed. Hard to imagine a crazier finish for the tournament and for us.

Before flying back to Charlotte, I had a final surprise for them. Reynolds was celebrating his 12th birthday on the day we were flying home. The night before, I surprised him by having a bagpiper march us into dinner, as is custom in Scotland. The piper played "Happy Birthday," and we sang together. Priceless.

And one final memory from that trip in 1995 … Christopher took up the game with a passion after the Scotland trip and developed into a pretty good player. The experience hooked him.

Our family made a return trip to Wester Brewlands for the 1997 Open Championship that Justin Leonard won. Sally's best friend at Charlotte Country Day, Kasey Pryor, and Reynolds' best friend also at Country Day, Hunter Edwards, joined us, and I have several enduring memories from our trip.

The antithesis of our Davis Love III encounter happened as Sally, Kasey, Reynolds, and Hunter were asking players for their autographs during practice rounds. Most players happily accommodated our kids and many others who were doing the same thing. Midway through the back nine, we came across Tiger Woods playing a practice round. The kids asked him for an autograph, and he told them he would sign after he finished practicing. Our group and others walked the rest of the back nine with Tiger in anticipation of getting his autograph beyond the 18th green. The kids gathered along the walkway that players used to get to the clubhouse. Jo and I watched in utter shock as Tiger walked past all the kids waiting, without acknowledging them in any way. They were crushed, and Jo has never forgiven him. I think it was an indication of what was to come in later years.

A more painful memory from that Open came while walking the back nine and watching Ian Baker-Finch. I told Jo about his Open victory at Royal Birkdale and his subsequent struggles with his game. Standing beside the 15th tee as Baker-Finch prepared to hit his tee shot, I saw he was well over par. It was obvious from his

body language that he wanted to be anywhere but where he was, his confidence was battered. If he could have walked in, he would have. We saw him struggling to even address the ball to hit his drive, and it felt awkward watching him. Baker-Finch eventually signed for 92, and I felt for him. It had been hard to watch. I had always been a fan of his for how he carried himself on and off the course. He epitomized style and grace. A shell of the player he had once been, Baker-Finch didn't play another Open Championship and began to focus on television work. If anyone ever doubted how much of golf is played between the ears, Baker-Finch served as a painful reminder.

Jo and I attended the 1999 Open, which was being played in Carnoustie for the first time since 1975. The Wearns joined us again to play and see some of The Open. Jo and Debbie went home on Friday and Buck left on Sunday, leaving me to watch the final round from a great reserved seat in the big bleachers surrounding the 18th green.

Carnoustie has the well-deserved reputation as the fiercest links in Scotland, and watching The Open there reinforced the reputation. I was struck by how quiet it was during tournament play, because so few birdies were being made. Once in a while, a cheer would echo across the flat windswept property but it seemed the players were faced with a nearly impossible challenge.

It was rainy and cold for Sunday's final round, a generally miserable afternoon. I wandered the course, watching various players before heading to my seats for the finish. As the day unfolded, a Frenchman named Jean Van de Velde had taken control of the tournament. I didn't know anything about him. If you know golf, you know how Van de Velde's story ended. It was an epic collapse, and I had a great seat to see it unfold. Had I been there.

The weather worsened in the afternoon, a mist turning into a steady rain; however, remembering what I had missed by leaving the 1995 Open too early, I was determined to stick it out. Van de Velde had a three-stroke lead heading to the 18th tee, and I was miserable. The drama, I figured, was over, and I was cold and wet. My warm car beckoned. I decided to leave.

Reaching my car, I heard a collective groan rise from around the 18th green. I turned on the radio to hear the BBC coverage, and as I drove away from Carnoustie, I listened to what I was missing. Van de Velde had kicked away his lead in colossal fashion. I had been right there and I had left. Again. Driving away, all I could think of *again* was the old adage that "It ain't over 'till it's over."

～

Inevitably, as I sat reminiscing and taking in the beautiful photos from our many trips, these wonderful memories from the past always lost out. Ultimately, thoughts of Sally would become overwhelming and the storm in my mind would return. Still, I couldn't cry.

13

Faith, Family and Friends

As days turned into weeks, one of the things that began to weigh heavily on my mind and Jo's was our desire to find the most meaningful way to honor Sally's beautiful memory and her legacy of caring for others. It's not unusual to hear people speak of a friend or family member who has died, noting how they prioritized their life with their faith first, their family second, and their friends third. I wish I could say I lived my life that way before we lost Sally. I can't even say that's how I live every day now, but the example she set with her life permanently changed me and put me on a path to becoming a better person in every respect.

Her life was her testimony to her tremendous faith in God. I don't doubt that after attending Camp Courtney, she lived every second with those priorities firmly in place and in that order. We heard from many of her friends that during her time at Peace, Sally was witnessing her faith to anyone she thought might listen, with the hope of leading them to Christ.

About a month before her accident, Sally and I talked about this. She told me what she was trying to do, and while she was discouraged by the way some people responded she was determined to not give up on the people who mattered to her. She wanted to help those she thought needed help.

As is hopefully always the case, families want to find the most appropriate way to honor the memory of their loved one, and others often want to do something as well to remember the one they've lost. I knew we would find something important related to Sally and name it in her honor. It would not be a hasty decision, however.

I told Jo that we needed to be certain about what we did. I wanted to give it considerable thought before taking any action. In the immediate aftermath of the accident we asked that all memorial gifts be made to Camp Courtney, given it was where she had committed her life to Christ. The amount of gifts that followed in honor of Sally's memory were overwhelming and allowed Grace Covenant to make much-needed improvements to the camp. We knew in our heart that Sally would have wanted this. As another small, but very personal way of honoring her memory, I ordered a personalized plate that reads MYSWTSAL.

Beyond our own contemplation, other well-intentioned friends and family offered their own thoughts of how best to accomplish honoring her memory beyond the memorial gifts to Camp Courtney. We wanted to do something that could cover all that was important to Sally, not just her church.

One suggestion to honor Sally shook me. After the girls' graveside service, we returned to our home and many followed. Shortly after our return, I was shocked when I was approached by someone who had also lost a loved one within the previous year. He mentioned how he planned to honor his loved one's memory and suggested we might want to take the opportunity to contribute and name Sally as well. I simply stared at him and couldn't comprehend how anyone would enter my home on this day with such an agenda.

As shocking as that suggestion had been, another touched me deeply. A year earlier I had built an eight-acre lake off the back of our home and put it into a conservation easement in the middle of a 70-acre plot of land. I included four neighborhood friends to whom I had sold property and developed the lake as a place for their families to fish and hike. Sally had often asked to visit the lake with me as it was being built, as did Randy Dorton, one of the friends involved in the project. I sought Randy's advice on the project, and he loved helping, especially because it gave him a diversion from the stress of his job with Hendrick Motorsports. When the lake was finished, Randy and Dianne loved to go there to enjoy the peace and quiet it offered.

On Easter Sunday, Randy and Todd Hamilton, whom I also involved in the lake project, asked me to ride there with them. When we got there, Randy told me the families involved had decided to name it Sally's Lake. They knew how much she loved it and they could not imagine it being named anything else. They planned to place a plaque next to the lake. However, in a few short months, another heartbreaking tragedy would ultimately determine the most appropriate name for it.

As time passed, people continued to approach us about plans to honor Sally's memory. I told them all the same thing—we hoped to find something that would capture all that was important to Sally. I had no doubt that in time God and Sally would reveal the right way to us. One night in June, the revelation came.

Around 3:00 a.m., I awoke and sat up in bed. With clarity and focus, I knew the most appropriate way would be to build a YMCA in eastern Lincoln County and name it for her. The Charlotte YMCA organization, unlike many Y organizations across our country, proudly and boldly embraces its Christian roots. Beyond this, no organization strives more diligently to provide a special place for family and friends and to help those less fortunate. The YMCA's mission shared the values that defined Sally and her life. The next morning I told Jo what I wanted to do, hoping she would agree. Without hesitation, she embraced the idea.

Since undergoing back surgery years before, I had made a habit of going to the Dowd YMCA in uptown Charlotte to work out on most weekday mornings. I planned that either before my workout or afterwards I would speak to Andy Calhoun, the YMCA of Greater Charlotte executive director, to share our wish. I had not previously met Andy and knew his office was located in another building. On my way in, I stopped at the front desk and asked where I might find him.

"He's standing right behind you," she said.

The serendipity of the moment struck me. There was no doubt we were doing the right thing. As I introduced myself, Andy said, "David, you need no introduction to me. You and your family have been in our thoughts and prayers. Many in our organization have been profoundly shaken by your loss. If there is anything we can do, please let us know."

I needed a moment to gather myself, and once I did, I told him about our desire to build a Y in Sally's memory, somewhere close to our home. Andy promised to talk with members of the YMCA board and get back to me.

As I walked in to start my workout, I continued to think about what had just happened. This was no chance meeting. God had placed us both here so that I could share our hope with Andy. It was clear that He has a plan for each of us. If I had doubts that His hands were leading me, they would be resolutely washed away soon.

14

SMC 12-9-84

~

Before the accident, Jo and I had planned a trip to Ireland. We had been to northwest Ireland the year before to play golf and sightsee. It had been a memorable trip, and we were looking forward to going back to now play some courses Jo had not played and a couple of new ones for me. Following the accident, Jo and I decided to take it a day at a time before deciding if we would still go. Beyond our own reservations, many of our friends tried to talk us out of going. They were worried about us being so far from home and having an emotional meltdown over Sally with no one there to support us.

Discussing our plans with Greg Currie one day, I mentioned that perhaps he and Jennifer might like to join us. We'd been to Scotland with them in 2000. As part of that trip, we also attended The Open where Tiger won his first Open. I knew they had never been to Ireland, but I also knew that Greg had recently started working with Johnny Harris, one of Charlotte's most prominent developers. I fully expected him to tell me they couldn't join us. To my surprise, Greg said they would love to come along.

In late June, the week following my discussion with Andy Calhoun, we flew to London and, from there, on to Belfast. Emotionally, I continued to struggle and felt our friends might have been right. Even with Greg and Jennifer along, I worried whether I could hold it together. While Quail Hollow was providing a quasi-private place to grieve on my own, the torrent of emotion inside my head continued to rage. There was little let up, and I didn't have any idea how I would eventually find peace in a life without Sally. No doubt Jo was experiencing many of the same feelings, but we had decided it might help to get away and spend time with Greg and Jennifer. Although this was intended to be a golfing vacation, I still had this nagging feeling that I didn't want to actually play golf. To the extent I could quantify the feeling, playing would involve pressure and I didn't want to feel any sense of pressure. I decided I would dig as deep as necessary to be able to play but would decline any attempt to place a wager, no matter how small.

We began our golf journey at Royal Portrush, an incredible championship links course that unarguably ranks as one of the world's greatest. The previous night we had checked into ArdTara Country House Hotel, which is forty-five minutes south of Portrush. We had never stayed there and found it to be the perfect place to begin our trip. The staff had been alerted to our loss and could not have been more accommodating to ensure our stay was enjoyable and stress free.

The next morning we drove to Royal Portrush. It had rained heavily overnight and more rain was forecast. A light rain was falling when we arrived at Portrush and, after checking in with the club secretary, we grabbed our clubs and donned our waterproofs—as rain suits are called in the Isles. The starter assigned us four caddies and we were off.

Jo, Greg, and Jennifer at Royal Portrush

As I stood on the first tee with Greg awaiting the starter's go-ahead to tee off, I looked at the Titleist Pro V1 in my hand. In the past, I always put two green dots underneath the logo on either side of the number, but thoughts of Sally came flooding in. I felt an overwhelming compulsion to mark my ball in some way that would be a tribute to her. *But ... would it be right to hit something that carried some recognition of her?* After what seemed liked hours, as I stared at my ball and held the green Sharpie to mark it, I slowly began to put SMC on one side and 12-9-84 on the other—Sally's initials and birthdate. The sense of doing this was overwhelming and powerful. As I marked the ball, it felt right. However, I had another ball in my pocket and decided not to mark that one. I considered that after a few holes, I might decide I couldn't continue to play the ball with Sally's initials and birthdate, or I might lose it. In either case, I would most likely want to return to my two green dots. I also wasn't sure how Jo would react to what I was doing. Even with these doubtful thoughts, I felt a sense of calm after I'd marked it.

The first hole is a relatively short par-4 to an uphill green. I remember my caddy suggesting I hit a long iron for placement rather than a driver, given it was cold and damp and we'd not hit any practice balls. I don't remember any other shots during that round, but I do remember hitting a perfect 3-iron to the center of the fairway and a 7-iron on the green for a two-putt par.

Amazingly, the weather held off for most of the round, but we left our rain suits on for good measure. Though I didn't play particularly well, I was pleased I finished the round without losing my ball. That doesn't happen often for me on links courses, especially one that's the caliber and difficulty of Royal Portrush. I was also relieved that even though Jo picked up my ball a couple of times to hand it to me, she did not see how I'd marked it. While it was still legible, the dampness and playing eighteen holes had worked on it. Yet, as pleased and relieved as I felt, I wasn't sure how to interpret that I had played the same special ball all day. I placed it in a separate pocket of my golf bag so I'd know where to find it.

The next day the weather cleared and the temperature was much warmer as we headed to Portstewart Golf Club. This was a new course for me. We ended up with three great caddies, the oldest a retired police officer. As we were preparing to play, I had to decide whether to play with a new ball or pull the one from the day before out of the side pocket. It was a small thing, but it felt like an enormous weight. I thought about having just played one of the toughest courses in the world with one ball that carried personal meaning for me. *Should I just keep it?* In all likelihood I would lose it here. I decided to play it and accept whatever happened.

The first is a solid downhill golf hole with massive dunes on the right covered in gorse, or whin, as it is called by many. Beyond the whin is the Atlantic Ocean. As I placed the ball on the tee and saw Sally's initials, I felt my heart in my throat and struggled to compose myself. I forced myself to focus, knowing Jo, Greg, Jennifer, and the caddies were all looking at me. No one knew about my golf ball, and I did not want to call attention to it by losing my composure at that moment. I remember walking away for a moment to gather myself while I kept my back toward everyone. Again, I managed to hit a perfect tee shot down the middle with my driver and then an 8-iron into the green. I two-putted for par.

On the second green, Jo picked up my ball to hand it to me and froze as she saw what was written on it. With a look of horror and anger she said, "How can you hit a golf ball with our daughter's initials and birthdate on it?" Greg and Jennifer acted like they didn't hear her and started walking to the third tee. The caddies did the same, as they had no knowledge of our loss or the meaning of what Jo had just said to me. I told Jo that I really couldn't say why but this felt like my own small tribute to Sally. I wanted to do it. However, I did not tell her that it was the same ball I'd played the day before.

I knew I'd upset her. I wasn't sure what else she might say about what I was doing, but I knew I wouldn't change my golf ball. I played inconsistently and just broke 90, but I never lost my ball, despite hitting it in some spots where I had little expectation of finding it.

Walking off the 18th green, I felt a sense of awe that I'd just played two very difficult courses with the same golf ball. I could not remember playing two courses there and not losing at least a couple of balls. Internally, I struggled to process what this meant but kept it to myself. Jo said very little to me the rest of the round and did not bring up the ball again.

After returning to our hotel that afternoon, Jo fell apart and cried uncontrollably over Sally. It was only the second time she'd broken down in my presence. Knowing what she'd been carrying since the night of the accident and what she had done to protect me with her amazing courage, I felt horrible. While she never said so, I knew my ball contributed to her feelings. I really didn't know what I would do for the remainder of our golf trip.

The following day we went to Giants Causeway near Bushmills to sightsee rather than play golf. It was a good thing because it rained most of the day. Afterwards, we drove to Newcastle to spend the night before playing Royal County Down the next day.

When we awoke the following morning, the sun was out and the temperature was mild, a beautiful Irish day. I had played County Down once and considered it one of my favorite courses anywhere, easily in my personal top five. It has been ranked the best course in the world on some global lists, and I was excited to play there again.

At the first tee, I again found myself facing the same uncomfortable question: *Do I continue playing the Titleist with Sally's markings on it or do I put it in my bag for safekeeping, a deeply personal souvenir for myself?* Given Jo's reaction at Portstewart and what had happened that afternoon, I was even more conflicted. But I felt a strong sense that I should continue using the same ball, letting it lead me wherever it seemed destined to take me. After two rounds, the markings were barely legible. If you didn't know what they were, you wouldn't have been able to decipher them at that point.

The first hole at County Down is a decent par-5, with Dundrum Bay running down the right side and a group of high dunes in play off the left side of the fairway. I wasn't as fortunate off the first tee at County Down as I had been at Portrush and Portstewart. I pulled my drive well left onto a huge dune, and based on how high up the dune and how dense the vegetation, I felt certain I had lost the ball. I felt sick but I did my best not to show any emotion.

To my shock and relief, my caddie found the ball and I was able to hack it back into the fairway. I don't remember my score on the first hole that day, but it was the first time I sensed that something larger than life was taking place. The ball should have been lost more than once, but I continued to find it.

From there, thoughts of Sally were ever present in my mind. I struggled to stay engaged in the golf but didn't want Greg, Jennifer, and Jo to sense what I was dealing with. I'd like to say I played well but I didn't. More importantly to me, despite hitting my golf ball into places where it might have been lost, I always managed to find it.

I had now played three of the most demanding courses in the world, the conditions different every day, and I had played all 54 holes with the same ball. I began to think Sally was there with me.

Greg, Jennifer, Jo and me on the ninth hole at
Royal County Down

After again spending the night outside Newcastle, we headed south to play County Louth, which the locals call Baltray. I wasn't sure what to expect, but I had been intrigued by Donald Steel's comment in his book, in which he said it would be a mistake to pass by County Louth while driving from Royal County Down to Portmarnock. Mr. Steel's endorsement convinced me to add it to our itinerary.

Another change in the weather—cooler with rain showers—made me wonder if I should put this ball into play again. I kept it to myself, but when I arrived at County Louth I had the same feeling I'd had at County Down. I wanted to let the ball lead me where it would.

While Jo and Jennifer put their clubs on trolleys, Greg and I took caddies who were as into our games as we were. Greg and I weren't playing for any stakes but the caddies didn't care. On one hole, Greg's caddie pointed out that I had inadvertently teed up in front of the markers and suggested the penalty be called. Instead, we just laughed about it. Over the course of the round I consistently played well and finished with the ball still in my possession, avoiding any real scares during my round. Something was definitely happening.

After spending a couple of days near Sligo, we headed off to Lahinch, one of the great Irish links where we were greeted by 30-mile-per-hour winds with higher gusts. The forecast was discouraging—the wind was expected to strengthen. We considered not playing, but because I was the only one in our group who had been there we decided to brave the elements.

As we stood on the first tee waiting to tee off, I faced the same question again—should I put the same charmed golf ball in play on such a rugged day or not? After being used for 72 holes, Sally's birthday and initials were practically invisible, but I knew they were there. I hadn't mentioned the ball again to anyone since Jo had confronted me about it at Portstewart, so no one had realized my growing obsession with keeping the ball.

I couldn't believe I had played four of the greatest links courses in the world without losing a ball, especially *this* ball. I struggled to comprehend what this might mean. Like the light that filled my car on the ride to Sea Island, I had a growing sense that God and Sally's hands were involved. I didn't know what they were trying to tell me, only that there was a message.

On a calm day, Lahinch with its dunes and deep rough is a stern test. In the wind, it would be a challenge for anyone to play the same ball for 18 holes. I felt sure I would lose the ball if I played it. As I gathered myself to hit my tee shot, I could not ignore the feeling that Sally was there and wouldn't leave me. I had to play this ball. Still, I understood every shot I hit could be the last I played with it. One errant swing and I might never see the ball again. As often happens when we try *not* to do something, fate strikes. As I made contact with the ball, I knew I had pulled it. Coming up, I could see it was headed toward the rough between the first and second fairway. My heart sank. I continued to watch until it landed. Thankfully, I could see it and breathed a huge sigh. I made a bogey from there, but it wasn't my score that concerned me any longer. It was holding on to this ball. I had 17 more holes to go—some of them extremely difficult. They would be 17 of the most challenging holes I would ever play.

The third hole at Lahinch is a great golf hole. The fairway is elevated above the tee and significant rough occupies most of the left side with the parking lot for the beach area just beyond it. It is a challenging driving hole even without wind. Again, I pulled my tee shot and it headed right toward the parking lot. My heart again sank as I thought I had indeed lost it. However, the wind held it up and it fell short of the parking lot into the deep rough. Still, I was in a near panic, waiting for Jo and Jennifer to hit their tee shots so I could go in search of it. To my amazement and great relief, I found it once more.

The wind was ferocious, and it was particularly difficult on Jo and Jennifer. They struggled to stand still enough to hit their shots. It was almost comical the way shots were careening in different directions, blown away by the relentless wind.

As a rule when Jo and I play, I stand and watch her shots to note anything about her swing and mark where her balls land—and help her find them if they're errant. On this day, however, I was so focused on what I was doing that I failed to offer my support, leaving her to search for her shots with her caddie. I didn't see the storm brewing inside her due to my absence. Waiting on the seventh tee for the fairway to clear, we sat down to get out of the wind as best we could. As only Jo can do, she told me to "go fly a kite," or something like that, and left to sit with her caddie. I offered to help her the rest of the day, but the look she gave me made it clear I could go my own way. She didn't stand with me for a picture and kept her distance the rest of the round. Greg and Jennifer tried to act as peacemakers, but there was no fixing out there what I had created. I would have to find a way when we got back to our hotel. For the rest of our round, I knew my focus was on trying not to lose this ball that was increasing in its meaning to me as we finished each hole. We continued to play through the wind, which worsened as our round progressed, only adding to the general misery of the day. More than once I thought I'd lost my ball, but I continued to find it.

On the 18th tee, I stood alone and reflected on all that had happened to get me to this place. After so many days of being unable to cry, I felt the tears coming as I waited to play the final hole of our trip. *Not now,* I thought, knowing that if I started crying here, I wouldn't be able to stop. All that had been building up since that night on the curb in Birkdale wanted to come gushing out, but I fought back the urge.

I came to another realization in those moments. *This is where I can grieve on my own.* I could let my feelings wash over me on these courses, an ocean away from home and friends, and I could somehow connect to Sally. I wouldn't have to worry about others watching me. Here, I might find a bit of peace through the pain. Suddenly, I understood that playing all this golf with the same ball had happened for a reason. It was Sally's sweet way of helping me find the place I desperately needed in order to gain whatever peace I could over losing her. There was no other way I could make sense of what had been happening.

As the wind continued to blow, I willed myself to focus on the task at hand. I still had to finish the round. One more hole to go with that same ball. Beyond finishing, I also knew I had to make things right with Jo as soon as possible.

The 18th at Lahinch can be played as a short par-5 or a long par-4. I don't remember how we played it that day. My sole focus was on keeping my golf ball. The wind was howling right to left, bringing deep rough that runs along the left side of the fairway into play along with a road that runs parallel to it. As someone who had spent years fighting to control a pull-hook that could rear its head at the worst possible moment, it was a terrifying shot.

I considered hitting an iron off the tee to assure I kept my ball in play, but my caddie handed me my driver before I had a chance to ask for it. *Please God,* I asked silently, *don't let me lose this ball now.* I was in a fragile emotional place and losing the ball now, after being with me consistently through multiple courses, might devastate me. There was little doubt Sally was here, and losing this ball on the last hole would crush me. It would be like losing her a second time.

Just as I feared, I pulled my tee shot. I watched in horror as my ball headed directly toward some of the deepest, thickest rough on the hole or, even worse, across the road to the left of the fairway and rough. Everything I was beginning to understand about this trip and Sally's ball might all be going away right there with one fateful swing. As I watched, it fell just short of the road and dove into the thick rough. I wanted to run immediately after my ball, my eyes locked on where I thought it had landed, but Jo, Jennifer, and Greg hadn't hit their tee shots. As had happened many times previously during this trip, with the awareness of the significance this ball was beginning to have to me, I was in total panic.

Once everyone had hit, I almost sprinted toward where I thought I would find it. I couldn't. The ball wasn't where I expected it might be, and a sense of despair began to hit me like a wave blindsiding me. *What if I've lost the ball on my last hole?*

Then I saw a ball that was barely visible in the tangle of grass. It was mine. I'll never forget the range of emotions that rushed through me. It didn't matter that my ball was unplayable. I had found it. That's all that I cared about.

I picked it up and clutched it in my hand as I processed what it meant to me. Again, as on the tee for the first time since the accident, as I held and looked at this ball, I could sense tears welling up in my eyes. I knew I couldn't allow myself to cry at this moment, and I willed myself to calm down before dropping the ball where I could hit a short iron into the fairway. From there, I hit a series of short shots to make sure I kept the ball where I could see it. On the green, I casually putted out, but again barely winning a wrestling match with my emotions. I pulled the ball out of the hole for the final time and tucked it into my pocket. I knew I would never play another hole with it.

We put our clubs in the car and headed off to the club's bar for a celebratory pint before driving back to Dromoland Castle where we were staying. Jo hardly looked at me. She spoke to me only if she had to. I hadn't told her the whole story, and the tension between us was impossible for Jennifer and Greg to ignore.

Back at Dromoland Castle, Jo said she was tired and would not be down for dinner. In the room, I told her I needed to explain what had happened. She said she was going to bed, but she was willing to listen. I told her about the golf ball and how, after all the golf we had played, I was determined not to lose the ball at Lahinch. "You might not understand," I told her, "but I felt Sally was there."

I reminded Jo of how Palmer Trice had told us we would grieve together and we would grieve apart. Marking the ball the way I had allowed me to feel a connection to Sally and was a way I could deal with my grief. I expressed to Jo how much I loved her and how sorry I was for leaving her on her own at Lahinch. I hoped she could forgive me and understand what I was telling her. She said it helped to hear my explanation and she asked me to leave her alone so she could process all I had told her. Greg and Jennifer had already headed downstairs for dinner, so I told Jo I would only go down for a moment to apologize for the discomfort I had created.

Understanding our emotions were raw, Greg and Jennifer could not have been more understanding. They were there for us, they explained, but they were also having a memorable time in Ireland. They were amazed when I told them about the golf ball.

When I returned to our room awhile later, I found Jo asleep. I didn't know when or how I'd tell her, but I was certain that this part of the world I had always loved was now where I'd have to come to find whatever peace I could over losing my sweet Sally. Sally's spirit was here and would be waiting on me. That's the only way to explain how I'd managed to play five of the most difficult courses in the world with the very ball I marked with her initials and birthdate on the first tee at Royal Portrush.

15

I Finally Cried

~~

The day after returning from Ireland, I headed to the Dowd Y to work out. Alone as I drove Highway 16, I thought about our trip, the golf ball, and, of course, Sally. As I drew closer to Charlotte, the storm that had been brewing inside me finally took its toll. Suddenly, I began to cry. Soon, I was sobbing uncontrollably. Three months of keeping it all inside came pouring out, and I couldn't stop.

Rather than go to the Y, I drove past it. There was little chance I could go there and headed instead to Quail Hollow. I knew I needed a place to be alone. At Quail, I could find a parking place away from everyone and sit in my car until I composed myself. I pulled into the lot above the 18th green and parked at the lower end, away from the building. I don't remember how long I was there, but it was at least a couple of hours. I just sat in my car and cried. My heart ached for Sally. I wanted to hug her and hear her sweet voice say my name. Yet, I knew she was gone and these things would never happen again.

After regaining my composure, I went to the locker room and showered before going to the veranda with my golf books. Alone, I reflected on our trip, particularly the feelings I'd had on the 18th tee at Lahinch. If there were any doubts that I needed to find a way and place to process the loss of Sally, what had just happened took care of them. I had no doubt that if I hoped to find the peace and acceptance God might grant me, it would happen by losing myself on golf courses in a part of the world I loved and where no one would know me.

Thinking of where, I picked up Donald Steel's book to review the courses he had listed. Since my first trip in 1986, I determined I had played 25 of the 75 courses Mr. Steel highlighted in his book. I was one-third of the way through his list, leaving 50 new ones to play.

The more I looked at the photographs and read what Mr. Steel wrote in his description of each course, especially of those I hadn't played, the more convinced I became that his book provided a roadmap for me to follow. By using the list of courses I hadn't played, I saw a path of golf holes I could walk—where I could truly lose myself playing the links courses I loved so much. This would be my long walk back to the living. I only hoped Jo would understand.

When I shared with her what I wanted to do, she could not have been more supportive. She knew how much I loved golf in the British Isles, and she understood how much I needed to find something and some way to grieve on my own. Given my emotional meltdown earlier in the day, I told her I hoped to go in the fall to play.

Jo then told me that she, Anne, and Katie wanted to take a trip of their own on the first anniversary of the girls' deaths. We also talked about doing something to show our gratitude to the Curries, the Browns, and the Dortons for all they had done for us after the accident, and we decided to rent a home in Tuscany for a week the following summer and invite them to join us.

That was what we would do for our friends. But I wanted to do something for Jo. I owed so much to her for how she sheltered me from having to identify the girls at the crash site and for so many other things she had done in the blurry, anguished days after the accident. Without telling Jo why, I began bringing her roses each week, just like the ones I began taking to Machpelah. It was a small way for me to express my immense love and gratitude for all she had done.

⁓

Having found my way to grieve, I still struggled to understand why God had taken Sally and Grace from us. It remained an unanswered question that wouldn't go away. After the accident, I had been approached by clergy connected with Christ Church and others who offered me spiritual help should I want it. I politely declined.

Now, though, I felt an urgent need to speak with someone with the hope of gaining some understanding of this. I decided to contact Associate Rector Lisa Saunders with Christ Church. Lisa had reached out on the day of the accident and offered to help in any way possible. While Lisa did not deliver the sermon Easter Sunday that included mention of the girls, I had always found something uplifting in her message and thought she could help me more than anyone else there. Upon reaching Lisa, I told her of my struggle to understand why God would have taken Grace and Sally from us. I missed Sally tremendously. She was my only daughter and that made ours a special relationship. Why was she gone? Why had God worked that way?

Lisa told me there are no easy answers as to why God would allow something so painful and horrendous to happen; however, I must trust that they are now with Him and in no pain. She told me that they are smiling down but bothered that our families are suffering because of their absence. She told me she wished she could offer words that would help ease my pain and said she would add to her personal prayer list a prayer that someday I would be blessed with a granddaughter as a way to fill the void left by losing Sally.

16

Sally's Y

In late August, I heard from Andy Calhoun. He wanted us to come to his office to speak with current board chair Jim Morgan to discuss our plans. I knew of Jim through mutual friends who thought highly of him, but we had never met previously. Interestingly, I would later discover while working on my family's heritage and history that our respective great grandparents had been close friends. While reading a newspaper account of my grandparents Clark's wedding in Williamston, South Carolina, the story noted that Mr. and Mrs. James Morgan, Jr., Jim's great grandparents, were the official greeters at the reception.

Jim began the meeting by telling us that he and his family had been praying for us. They had been deeply affected by our loss. I knew he meant it. He was clearly a man of integrity who was not hesitant to share his deep Christian faith. When he led us in a prayer, I listened to his words and felt again that God had led us here.

Andy asked me to share with Jim our vision for building a Y in Sally's memory. As I started to speak, the tears began to flow. Since that morning in mid-July when I cried for the first time after the accident, any mention of Sally brought them on. As best as I could while the tears flowed, I explained that the most important thing in Sally's life was her faith. She had found Christ at a Christian summer camp following eighth grade, and it defined her until the end. I told Jim how she prioritized her life first with her faith, then her family came second, and her friends were third. It was important to us to find the most meaningful way to honor those priorities and to continue her beautiful legacy of helping and caring for others, yet we were determined not to rush into a decision on how best to do this in the aftermath of accident.

I described how, in June, during the middle of the night, I awoke with clarity and focus that the most appropriate and meaningful way to honor Sally's life and priorities was to build a new Y in our community and name it after her. I told them I didn't know what was required or precisely how we'd do it, but I had no doubt we would get there. As a starting point, I felt my family would be willing to donate land, and Jo and I would also make a substantial financial gift to get things started.

Andy and Jim were visibly moved by our desire to honor Sally in this way. They shared our view that we could make it happen. Andy then told us that as an indication of the support we could expect, two families—the Cummings and the Keiths—after hearing through others that we might decide to do this, had communicated to the Y leadership their willingness to financially support our vision should we move forward to do it.

Jo and I were overwhelmed. Neither of us had spoken to either family about our decision and to hear of their unilateral desire to support it was just another sign of how Sally had touched so many lives. Her hands and God's were moving us in the right direction.

Andy explained that a feasibility study would be required to determine the interest in supporting the construction of a Y in our area. However, because the entire Charlotte YMCA community was in the midst of an ongoing capital campaign, the timing of the study and any initiation of efforts to raise money would need to be delayed until the capital campaign was completed later this year. I, in turn, asked them to do whatever was necessary to satisfy the Y's board and leadership as soon as feasible. While disappointed that our vision would be delayed we were prepared to commit whatever time was needed to help see it become a reality. We began to refer to our vision as Sally's Y.

17

Trying to Find
A New Beginning

Our family, individually and collectively, in the months that followed tried to find a way to somehow move forward and find a new beginning. For me, with my decision to make my way back to the British Isles to grieve, I began to plan a trip. My ability to do so was made possible by changes in my job with my family. Those changes were initiated first with the passing of my mother in 1991 and then my father in 1997. To help settle their estates, some of my family's real estate holdings that had been my responsibility were sold.

As anyone who has been involved with a family business knows, while there are many blessings to them, there are equally as many challenges that can create an enormous amount of stress. The pressure of these challenges had taken its toll, and when the opportunity to move our remaining interests to a third party came along in 2002, I recommended to my family that we accept it. Over the next year-and-a-half, I implemented the plan and completed it near the end of 2003. For the first time since I left Carolina in 1978, I was free of everyday business responsibility.

As I look back on that move, God's hands were already at work. He knew there would be little chance I could overcome losing Sally and Grace the next spring if I also had the challenges of my job. The combination of the two would have been too much. While there remained shared real estate holdings with my two brothers and sister, those did not require everyday oversight. With the absence of those daily responsibilities, my ability to head back to the British Isles at the time of my choosing became possible.

With Jo's blessing, I began putting together a late-September-early-October trip of 10 courses on my list in the southern part of England. However, as friends became aware of my plans, many implored me not to go. Susan Brown, who had held us up following the accident—along with her husband, Ronny, the Curries, and the Dortons—reminded me what had happened on my Sea Island trip. After some reflection, I knew she was right and decided to wait until the following summer.

Shortly after we returned from Ireland, Jo decided to lead a bible study group that fall. She continued to see this as a way to process her personal grief on her own by immersing herself in her deep and growing faith and among those who shared it. She also remained the pillar of strength for our family.

We also extended the invitation to our friends who stayed by our side to join us the following summer in Tuscany and all accepted. Randy's availability would depend on the race schedule, but he hoped to still make it. Dianne would definitely be there. Given that the house we secured had seven bedrooms, we also invited Jo's sister Anne, Grace's mother, and Katie, her only other daughter. We also included Greg's brother Pat and wife, Nan, to come as our guests. They had gone with us in 2000 to Scotland to play golf and watch The Open. I decided also to plan my golf around our time in Tuscany.

Since their first date the night of the accident, Reynolds and Jennifer began to date regularly. Beyond their romantic interest in one another, Jo and I believed that the shared loss of a sibling drew them even closer. In each other we thought they would find a soul mate to process their own grief and heartbreak. Reynolds also transferred to N. C. State to pursue a degree in forestry. While this was already in the works before the accident, I'm sure the change in schools helped provide a new start from the lingering memories of that night.

Even though Graham shared little with us about how he was handling the loss of Sally, he had a wonderful group of friends and family that did everything imaginable to spend time with him and provide support. We did, however, decide at the end of the school year that a change in schools could be a good move. Additionally, since the first grade, he had attended a private school that helped children overcome learning challenges. Over the six years he had been there, he made steady progress and his teachers thought he was ready for a mainstream school. Beyond friends at his current school, many others attended Charlotte Country Day. In particular, Lee Cummings, one of his closest friends, went to school there. Sally and Reynolds had also gone there, and we decided to enroll him as well.

Additionally, our family had been in the same home for nearly 20 years. While Jo and I had already been thinking of selling it as we moved toward the status of "empty nesters," the presence of so many special memories there with Sally was too much, and we committed to sell it. Individually and collectively, our family began to seek a new beginning and a new normal. Then life and its heartbreak interrupted our world again.

18

It Can Always Be Worse

T here are things worse in life than losing a child. Losing more than one child or multiple members of your family at once is worse.

The world has a way of providing perspective—both good and bad—and it did so on October 24, 2004. I received a call late that afternoon from a neighbor who asked if I was watching television. I wasn't, so he shared the news of an apparent crash involving a plane from Hendrick Motorsports en route to Martinsville, Virginia, for the NASCAR race. My neighbor feared Randy Dorton was on the plane, but he wasn't certain. The news stunned me.

One day earlier, I had spoken with Randy, who was home celebrating his wedding anniversary with Dianne. They had taken a bottle of wine and gone to Sally's Lake to celebrate. *Please don't let this be true,* I thought.

Jo and I went to be with Dianne and headed to their home. By the time we arrived, several cars were already in the driveway. We found Dianne in their bedroom surrounded by friends. While waiting with her, she received a call confirming the worst—the plane had crashed and there were no survivors. Randy had been on the plane. He was gone. I was in shock and felt sick. I told Jo we needed to leave. I wanted to help Dianne the way she and Randy had helped us, but it was still too raw for me. Randy had been Dianne's life. She was inconsolable. They had met at a race in Sonoma, California, fallen in love and been married shortly thereafter. They were as devoted to each other as a couple could be. And suddenly on a Sunday afternoon their lives had been torn apart forever. We hugged Dianne and left, hoping the other friends could help her in the same way she had helped us through our heartbreak.

Back home, I watched the news, and when I saw the list of victims, I was stunned. I had lost a great friend and felt devastated. However, I couldn't imagine what Rick Hendrick, the team owner, and his family were going through. They had lost their son Ricky, Rick's brother John, and John's two daughters, along with other members of the Hendrick Motorsports family. I knew Rick and Randy were incredibly close and had been together since Rick had started his race team. I remembered times when I had been with Randy and he was on the phone with Rick. He always ended his calls the same way, saying, "Love you, boss man."

We were still dealing with our grief and then this happened. Dianne lost her husband, I lost a great friend, and Rick Hendrick lost so many people dear to him. It was a cruel reminder to me that things could always be worse.

At the Dowd Y the next morning, I ran into Tom Sorensen, the sports columnist for the *Charlotte Observer*. I approached Tom and introduced myself. I told him it was understandable that the attention in the aftermath of this tragedy would focus on the Hendrick family, but I asked Tom not to forget Randy. Tom thanked me for sharing my feelings and asked if he could call me later to talk about Randy. When he did, I shared the details of my own loss and what Randy and Dianne had done for us. He asked me to describe Randy. "He was a friend's friend," I told Tom. Someone you could count on when you needed him. That was Randy Dorton.

I decided that Sally's Lake needed to become Randy's Lake. He loved going there, and I felt it was the right thing to do. I also made the decision to build another lake on our property. It would become Sally and Grace's Lake, a place we have come to love.

I put plaques to honor Randy and the girls at their respective lakes. Randy's monument is at the upper end of Randy's Lake, and the girls' plaque is on a large rock overlooking Sally and Grace's Lake. The girls' plaque reads:

Sally and Grace's Lake
This lake is dedicated to the memory of our sweet daughter,
Sally, and beloved niece, Grace, who tragically lost their lives in an
auto accident on April 4th, 2004. While they are no longer here with
us, we will never forget them and look forward to
our reunion with them in our Lord's Home. This lake and its won-
drous beauty is a reminder to how special these two girls
were and what they meant to those that knew them. We Love You

19

The First Step in Accountability

~⌣~

In November, after consulting with an attorney, Jo and I, along with Anne and Dick, filed a wrongful death lawsuit against the ownership of the bar where Shimp had been served six pints of beer and three shooters of liquor. The lawsuit wasn't about money. It was about accountability. Whatever we might be awarded would go toward the construction of the YMCA in Sally's memory. I also hoped our lawsuit would send a strong and loud signal to other bars and restaurants that they needed to be more careful in serving their customers so that other families could be spared what ours had endured.

In January 2005, we were told that Shimp planned to plead guilty to both counts of second-degree murder at his hearing, scheduled for early February. I could not forgive him but was grateful he was willing to take responsibility for his actions and spare us the pain and anguish a trial would bring. What Shimp chose to do was relatively rare and, to me, showed some remorse and maturity. The reality, though, assistant district attorney Marsha Goodenow told us, was that by pleading guilty, Shimp could avoid a potentially harsher sentence had he fought the charges and been found guilty. The evidence against him was overwhelming.

As Shimp's trial approached, I decided to drive Sally's car for the first time. It had not been moved since Dianne drove it home. The car still contained Sally's book bag, some of her favorite CDs, her favorite candy, and other familiar things she carried, along with her favorite jacket. I wasn't sure the car would start, but it did. I decided to drive it to Charlotte. I wasn't going anywhere in particular, but I wanted to be in her car. Again, I found myself talking to Sally, telling her how much I missed and loved her.

On Kings Road, just past Carolinas Medical Center, I pulled behind a car turning left. Looking through the windshield, my heart nearly stopped when I read the bumper sticker on the car. It read: *"Highways or Dieways: You Make the Choice."* I was stunned. The message was so wrong. Sally and Grace weren't given a choice. They had done everything right, while others, particularly Shimp, his friends, and the employees at the bar, had done so much wrong. They were still here, and Sally and Grace were gone.

As I continued driving, I knew we could not keep Sally's car. Being in it for the first time since her accident and seeing that bumper sticker was too much, so I headed immediately to Hendrick BMW. When I found Greg Hayes, I told him to sell Sally's car and to do everything humanly possible to arrange for it to go out of state so there was little chance Jo and I might see it on the road. Greg assured me he would do his best to honor my request. He remembered the day I brought Sally to the dealership to pick up her new car, and the memory brought both of us to tears. Greg sold the car and I never saw it again.

I saw Scott Shimp in person for the first time on February 7, 2005, the day of his plea hearing. I'd seen his photograph in the newspaper, but I'd never seen him in person. I'd hardly read about him, because the stories invariably mentioned Sally and Grace and often had a photo of Suzanne Kessler's Honda with a sheet covering it. I saw the car in my memory from that night and didn't need to see it in the newspaper.

The courtroom atmosphere was tense. Many of our friends and family had come to support us. His family was in the courtroom, too. Waiting for the hearing to begin, I prayed we wouldn't see more pictures of the accident or have to listen to much discussion about Sally and Grace. I wasn't sure I could keep my composure if we had to relive the details again. Marsha Goodenow reviewed the evidence and mercifully kept it to a minimum, anticipating Shimp's guilty plea. The police officers who testified focused on Shimp's condition at the accident scene rather than on what had happened to the girls.

After hearing their testimony, the presiding judge asked if anyone in our family wanted to speak. Jo, Anne, and Dick had asked that I speak for all of us. I had prepared a statement, hoping that I could contain my emotions long enough to get through reading it. When it came time for me to speak, the tears came and wouldn't stop.

As I continued to read through my tears, I looked across the courtroom and saw Shimp crying, too. I could hear many in both families crying as well. I told the court that he had made a number of bad choices that night, and that not only did we lose Sally and Grace, but his life would never be the same after what had happened. He would have to carry the heaviest burden a person could carry. I also told the court about driving Sally's car and seeing the bumper sticker. "The girls were not given a choice," I said, referring to its message. I told Shimp he had taken from us the most precious thing he could—our child. Because of his actions, he had denied me the opportunity to walk my sweet Sally down the aisle on her wedding day.

When Shimp took the stand, I listened in disbelief as he said he wasn't stumbling drunk that night, but that he should not have been driving. You cannot consume what he drank that night and not be nearly incapacitated. And why drive 90 miles per hour? Why? He then spoke of seeing Sally and Grace in the car after the wreck, who appeared to be asleep or unconscious. The knife of pain dug deeper into me. Had Shimp continued to speak, I would have been forced to leave. I couldn't hear any more.

When the hearing concluded, I was asked to speak with reporters. I told them our families had lost the most precious gift God grants us—our children—and we would forever miss them. A reporter asked me if our families felt Shimp had received the correct sentence. I told them we felt he was remorseful, but he had made some horrible decisions that night and had been properly charged. We didn't see Shimp as a hardened criminal, however, and saw no reason for him to spend the rest of his life in prison.

As we left the hearing, I told our attorney that we were prepared to do whatever was necessary to hold the bar accountable for what had transpired. We felt strongly the bar was almost as responsible as Shimp for taking Sally and Grace from us.

20

A Plaque to Remember

As planned, Jo, Anne, and Katie left in late March to be away over the first anniversary of the accident, and I stayed home. As I dropped them off at the airport, Jo asked what I planned to do. I told her I wasn't sure but that I would let my emotions guide me.

The morning of April 3, I went by Costco and bought roses and sunflowers to take to Machpelah and to place at the scene of the accident. I then drove to Quail Hollow and stayed at the back of the range hitting one practice ball after another, constantly thinking of Sally. Many times I just stared down the range and cried. As the day wound down, I headed to the veranda and again found a table away from the main seating area and had dinner alone. Afterwards, as I drove home, I cried practically the entire ride as I talked to Sally and told her how much I loved and missed her.

Before going home, I went to Machpelah to place roses and sunflowers. Walking to our family's plot, I felt my heart in my throat as I stared at the mound of flowers others had already placed there. Several notes had also been placed. I laid down mine and headed back to my car with tears streaming down my face. I wasn't ready to go Birkdale and headed home. There I just sat in a chair staring out the French doors off our bedroom, thinking of how our world had been torn apart a year ago. At 2:00 a.m., I decided to drive there to place the flowers where I thought the car had come to rest. As I drove, I remembered our frantic drive a year earlier along this same route. Driving down the hill toward the intersection, rather than seeing the crumbled up Honda, there was another mound of flowers. It was heartbreaking. I struggled with whether to stop, then pulled over, got out, and placed mine with the others. Notes had also been placed amongst the flowers. What I saw was a testament that people still remembered our girls and that their lives continued to mean something to others. I returned to my car and drove home, crying uncontrollably the entire way.

Several months earlier, I had ordered a plaque to place near where the girls' car had come to rest. I had been given permission from the owner of the property to place it there but still needed to get the same from the Huntersville Police Department. The previous week, I had received a call that it was ready for me to pick up. I'd then called the police department to see if it would okay for me to place the plaque at the accident site sometime the following week. They told me it would be fine. Later in the day, one of the officers on the scene the night of the accident called and said he'd like to join me when I placed the marker.

The morning of April 7, I picked up the plaque and drove to the accident scene. I was shocked and touched to see several Huntersville police cars there as well as one other car I didn't recognize. Three officers and a reporter from the *Huntersville Herald* had come to be with me. They asked to see the plaque, and I could see they were emotional as they read it.

On the plaque I had put:

"*Sally McKenzie Clark and Anna Grace Jordan tragically lost their lives here when the car they were riding in was struck by a drunk driver. These two girls were not only special children but special human beings. They brought much love and happiness to all who knew them and will be forever missed until we join them in heaven. This plaque is placed here to remind those who take time to read it that a life is precious and to consider the consequences before drinking and driving. Your decision to do so may not only put your life in danger, but others as well.*"

At the top of the plaque, I placed a sunflower.

When they finished reading, the officers moved their police cars into the nearest lane of traffic, turned on their flashing lights, and directed traffic around us. The officers then helped me carry the plaque to where they remembered that the car carrying Sally and Grace had come to rest. When we finished positioning the plaque so that it faced toward the road, I hugged each officer and thanked them for what they had done that night. I also noticed that they had placed their own reminder to those who came by. On the light post directly behind my plaque they put a sticker that read, "*Speed Shatters Lives.*"

As I prepared to leave, Tucker Mitchell, the reporter, asked to talk with me for a few minutes. Sitting in a nearby parking lot, he asked why I had decided to place the plaque. I told him that, like many people, I had passed roadside memorials left by loved ones and wondered why they'd done it. Now I understood. Grief and heartbreak move you to action. You want to remind others that lives were lost here. In our case, I believed the circumstances made our loss even more painful, because it could have been avoided. Shimp, his friends, the people at the bar, they all could have changed what happened but they didn't. "My hope," I said, "is that perhaps someone will read the plaque and decide not to drive after having too much to drink or will stop someone else from doing so." I had to try to keep something like this from happening again to someone else.

21

An Affirmation

~

After my decision not to go on my trip in the fall, I planned an itinerary that would allow me to play some before our time in Tuscany with our friends and family and then return after they left. Buck Wearn had asked to join me on the later trip, and we also decided to see The Open that was again going to be played over the Old Course in St. Andrews.

As I'd done the previous fall, I would again start in England, where more than half the courses on my list were located. I would play entirely there before joining our group in Rome. With Buck coming over for some of the second part in Scotland and The Open, I added courses I had previously played, knowing Buck would like to play them.

Beyond planning my golf, I wanted to find a way to honor Sally. It would be different than what I'd done with my golf ball in Ireland, but I needed to do something that would remind me why I was there. After much thought, I had a sunflower embroidered on my golf bag with "My Sweet Sally" stitched beside it. I wanted the same thing on my golf balls. Scott Davenport, the head pro at Quail Hollow, said he'd make it happen.

Beyond these purchases, knowing the amount of walking I would do, I decided to buy a pair of ECCO soft spike shoes. I had heard from several friends that they were the most comfortable shoes on the market. After purchasing them, I played several rounds and concurred—they were indeed the most comfortable golf shoes I'd ever had. However, I only wish I'd worn them while walking a course rather than riding in a golf cart.

Our trip to Tuscany was set. Dianne asked to bring her mother and sister, and we were happy to have them join us. They had flown in from California immediately after hearing of Randy's accident and had hardly left Dianne's side. With everything now in place for what was going to be a special trip, I flew to London on June 11 to begin playing and to start my search for the peace I so desperately hoped to find along my walk. It had been more than a year since Sally's accident, but the heartache remained just below the surface. I was anxious to finally have time to myself where I might find the space to grieve on my own. I missed Sally deeply.

The first course on my itinerary was Seacroft in the northeastern part of England. I picked up a rental car at Gatwick and headed to where I'd spend the night. The following day was overcast with temperatures in the 60s and little wind when I teed off at Seacroft in the early afternoon. The course seemed relatively quiet for a Sunday. As I stood on the first tee holding one of the golf balls I'd had personalized, and looking at my golf bag with a sunflower and the words "My Sweet Sally" stitched into the side, the tears began to come. While excited to be at Seacroft, I did not want to be here for the reason that had brought me. Both reminded me of why. With three women waiting to tee off behind me, I had to summon the strength to keep my emotions from overwhelming me. This was not the place to break down. I could only imagine what the women were thinking, as I could not entirely hide that I was crying.

I glanced at the Stroke Saver book I'd purchased in the golf shop to find my distances and way around the course, focusing my attention on the first hole description while I composed myself. I was playing the yellow member tees, as visitors were almost always asked to do on courses in the British Isles. Unlike in the States where, on most courses, you can choose the length of course you want to play, visitors are typically strictly forbidden from playing off the back tees—commonly referred to as the competition tees—without securing prior approval from the club pro, the secretary, or a member. Failure to do so will almost always bring a sharp rebuke by someone with the club.

The description noted that the first hole is a par-4 of nearly 400 yards, nicknamed Tree for the large tree behind the green. It's important to avoid a large fairway bunker with your tee shot. After folding and putting the book in my back pocket, I gathered myself as best I could and managed to hit a solid drive left of the fairway bunker. The feeling of relief was immense. I put my bag on my shoulder and off I went. I remember very little about the round other than my opening tee shot and my final score. I shot an 83.

The course didn't make a significant impression but my new shoes did. By the ninth hole, I had blisters on both heels from my new ECCOs. So much for how comfortable they had felt at home. Given the amount of golf I still hoped to play, I knew I would have to do something or my trip could be ruined. On my way back to my hotel, I stopped at a pharmacy—"chemists" in the U.K.—and got some Band-Aids, which they call plasters. I looked for Mole Skin but couldn't find anything of that sort, so I had to trust the Band-Aids to work, layering them on for maximum coverage and protection.

The next morning, I played Hunstanton, and took a caddie. He was a teenager but did a great job helping me break 80. The course remains a favorite, and not just because I drove the par-4 12th hole, which impressed him. However, the Band-Aids didn't work and my blisters worsened. With plans to play 36 holes a day for three days and 45 holes on a fourth day before heading to Rome, I was in serious trouble. At least my feet were. I found a larger version of the Band-Aids I was using and hoped they would help.

The next course was Great Yarmouth and Caister, an interesting course that's built around a horse track. On the first hole, you hit your tee shot over a portion of the track and then play your second shot over another part of the track. Not your average golf hole. In addition to the first hole, I remember the 4th and 11th as the best holes there. Though I don't recall my score, I do remember the Band-Aids finally providing lasting protection and felt encouraged that I might have found a way to protect my feet while they healed.

I then drove south to Felixstowe Ferry where the club secretary had asked to join me. Fortune smiled on me—more precisely on my feet—because we used a buggy, or what we call a golf cart. It was only the second time I'd done so when playing there. The first time was in 2003 with Jo at Enniscrone in Ireland, and we both agreed we'd never do it again. It was like riding a roller coaster on uneven tracks. True links courses are not built or designed for them. However, given the condition of my feet, I gladly accepted his offer.

I set myself up in a new hotel in southeastern England with the goal of playing six courses in the area. I started at Royal Cinque Ports, an excellent links course that had hosted two Open Championships early in the 20th century. I don't recall what I shot, but I do remember playing well and again driving a par-4 on the 10th hole, where a foursome was on the green as my ball landed short and ran off the back. I was afraid I might get an earful for hitting into the group ahead, but instead they turned and applauded. Still,

I apologized. Unfortunately, my blisters had become a problem again and I was running out of solutions.

I went next door to Princes Golf Club in the afternoon with the intention of playing all three nines at the club. My blisters were such a problem, I decided to play just two and return another time to play the third nine. I played the Himalayas and Shore but don't remember much else because the blisters were really bothering me.

I felt a sense of desperation setting in as I finished my round. I had so much more golf to play, but unless I could remedy the blisters I wondered if I could do it. Also, given my focus on my blisters on practically every hole, starting with the back nine at Seacroft, I really had not been able to spend time reflecting on what had brought me here. I was also beginning to feel maybe my presence here was a mistake, and God and Sally were now telling me so. As I loaded up my clubs and gingerly took off my shoes, I remembered a caddie on an earlier trip telling me the benefits of salt water when I'd mentioned blisters. As I drove away with the English Channel running along the left side of the road, and with nothing to lose, I decided to pull over and stand barefoot in the water for a few minutes. I rolled my pants up and waded in. The water was cold, but it felt good, and I stood there for about fifteen minutes looking out to sea. As I stood and reflected on the last few days and Sally, the tears began to flow and I asked Sally and God for guidance. I felt strongly I was where I needed to be and doing what I believed they had led me to do, but having to confront a problem of this nature at the beginning of my trip, I could not help but think I had it all wrong.

After returning to my car, I decided to pick up some Epsom salt on the way back to my hotel and soak my feet in the tub that evening. After soaking my feet, I had dinner, then went to the bar for a single malt. I asked the bartender if it would be okay for me to take off my shoes and put my feet on a chair, explaining my issue. He was fine with it, and I made sure he documented the moment by having him snap a photo.

As I sat there that evening, the thought of what had led me to this place was overwhelming. The tears again flowed. All of this could have been avoided. I looked out a window, so the couple sitting near me wouldn't notice me crying. I had only played six courses on my list, and I was facing the prospect of being unable to continue because of my blisters. Even if the salt water helped, I still had no way to protect my heels. I had developed another blister on my right big toe, and I had begun to worry about infection. I had brought two pair of golf shoes, but both were the same style EC-COs. I also had a pair of Nike running shoes, but I didn't consider them an option for golf, especially if it rained. I was running out of options.

The next morning, as I headed south toward Rye Golf Club, it seemed the salt water might have helped. I would just see how far I could go.

Rye is rich in tradition, and I thought of Donald Steel's comment that when he daydreamed about golf, he thought about Rye. That told me plenty. I had also read of how Oxford and Cambridge play an annual golf match at Rye for the Presidents Putter, a tradition that dates back to the late 1800s. As a general rule, the British speak of par-5s as long holes and par-3s as short holes. In Mr. Steel's book, he notes that at Rye there is only one long hole and five short ones, an unusual combination even for the sometimes quirky courses in the British Isles.

Many courses in the U.K. welcome visitor play because it can provide a significant revenue stream, allowing the clubs to keep member dues low. Rye, however, has a different approach and strictly limits guest play. Before I could play, I had to present myself to the club secretary and provide a letter of introduction, stating that I was a member in good standing of a club, and provide my handicap. This type of formality had been commonplace when I made my first trip in 1986. However, in recent years, many clubs have gradually stopped asking for it. Muirfield and Royal Troon are the only clubs that have asked for such documentation in recent trips. Nevertheless, I still carry a letter from Quail Hollow pro Scott Davenport just in case I'm asked for one.

As at Muirfield, a jacket is required to enter the clubhouse. I introduced myself to the secretary and provided my letter. He welcomed me and told me he had arranged for Vic Booth, one of the club's best caddies, to go out with me.

I put on my shoes and carefully made my way to the golf shop across the road. My blisters, though better, were still tender and painful. I had to find a way to ease the pain or I knew I would not be able to continue.

I hit it off with Vic immediately. Before we headed out, I went into the shop to see if there might be anything for my blisters.

While in there, I noticed a shoe display in the shop with another style of ECCOs called Hydromax. They were among the ugliest golf shoes I'd ever seen and cost nearly 150 pounds, but they were waterproof. I asked the assistant pro about the shoes, and he told me they were new but very popular among the members who had purchased them. I had nothing to lose other than about 150 pounds, so I bought the shoes. Immediately, as I stood in the golf shop, I knew my feet were in a better place. The relief was instantaneous, as there was no pressure on my blisters. These shoes seemed heaven sent. I still have them and take them on every trip. They've become my go-to shoes regardless of the weather. Tony Cunningham at Quail Hollow, who takes care of the locker room with his brother Calvin, manages to bring them back to life no matter how wet and worn they become.

As we went around Rye, I learned Vic was an accomplished golfer, a 1-handicap who had won some local competitions. He had retired from law enforcement and caddied on occasion. When I told him what had brought me here, he was visibly moved and recalled several cases involving the death of a child he had investigated that were heartbreaking. As we made our way around the course, we talked life and golf. It reminded me of my time on the range at Quail Hollow with Eric.

My round at Rye remains among my most memorable. Beyond the decision to buy the shoes and my time with Vic, I fully appreciated the comments Mr. Steel made about Rye. I believe it is a course any golfer can enjoy playing regularly.

With my new shoes, I knew I could continue my trip. The timing of this, given my moment of reflection and doubt just the day before, reaffirmed my decision to come here in search of God's peace over losing Sally. Rejuvenated, I played Royal St. Georges in the afternoon. Though it's a great course, I don't remember much about it. After finishing, I returned to my hotel and again soaked my feet in Epson salt.

The next day I went 36 again, this time at Littlestone Golf Club, then at Hayling Island Golf Club. When I was finished, I headed toward a hotel near Gatwick Airport for my trip to Rome to join Jo and our friends. As I drove, I reflected on the fact that in six days I had played 10 of the 50 courses I had set out to play and when I returned in two weeks, I could check off another six. It was a gratifying start, but a year after Sally's accident, and even with Shimp's acknowledgement of guilt, I didn't feel any closer to finding peace with what had happened. My heart still hurt, almost as much as it had that horrible night. After the episode with the blisters, I knew I was where I needed to be. However, I began to wonder what it would mean if I played all the courses in Mr. Steel's book and failed to find the closure I was seeking by the time I finished. As I flew to Rome the next day, I pulled out the AA's golf course guide I had purchased the year before. It was one of the books I had taken with me to the veranda at Quail Hollow—a compilation of more than 2,500 courses throughout the British Isles. It breaks down the courses by county and town, and provides contact information, directions, and other pertinent information, such as who designed the course and the standard of golf to be expected. Using terms common in the British Isles, it also provides a description of the type of course each is considered. Most courses listed fell in the category of links, seaside, clifftop, heathland, and parkland. The first three are almost always on the coast, or at least that's where they should be. As I looked through the book, I made note of those courses that were described as a links course. Some I had heard of; others I had not. The descriptions were generally brief, but I had a growing sense that there were many more courses beyond the list provided in Mr. Steel's book. If I needed more holes to walk, I knew I'd find them here.

Arriving in Rome, I went looking for our group, most of whom had arrived an hour before me. I found Dianne, her mother, Deon, and her sister Andy. When I asked where Jo was, they had a devilish look in their eyes. I immediately suspected something was up. I found out as soon as I saw Jo. For reasons known only to her, she had put a red streak in the front of her hair that reminded me of Herman Munster's wife, Lily. I was speechless. Jo, amused by my befuddlement, asked me what I thought, and all I could say was "interesting."

Over the next week-and-a-half, we had one of the most enjoyable and memorable trips imaginable. There were moments of emotion for everyone when memories of Sally, Grace, or Randy entered the conversation. The most difficult moment probably came when we decided to have a group photo taken in one of the many sunflower fields scattered across Tuscany. It was a beautiful setting, but it was also a gut-wrenching reminder of why we were all there together.

Most of our group in the sunflower
field in Tuscany

After the rest of the group headed home, Jo and I headed to the Amalfi coast area and Capri. We'd always wanted to go there, and this was the right time to do it. We had a wonderful time but often found ourselves thinking of Sally and how much she would have loved being there. She loved sunsets, and we saw one beautiful one after another.

22

It Will Take Longer

~

Following our time there, Jo flew home and I returned to London to continue playing courses on my list. On the night before flying to Rome, I had left my clubs in England, and they were waiting for me at the hotel on my first night back. Before heading to Scotland to meet Buck, I planned to first fly to the Isle of Jersey and then to the Isle of Guernsey to play Royal Jersey, La Moye, and Royal Guernsey. I would then take a ferry back to mainland England, drive to northwest England, and play a few more before flying from Manchester to Inverness to meet him.

The next morning when I reached the airline counter at Gatwick Airport, I was stunned to learn that I had to pay nearly 200 pounds in excess baggage fees because my luggage weighed more than 50 pounds per bag and I'd exceeded their quota for checked bags. I'd had no such issue leaving the U.S. and didn't feel I should be penalized now; however, the airline wouldn't budge. If I was going to make my flight, I had to pay the baggage surcharge. It was an expensive lesson but one that forever changed the way I pack for overseas trips. Instead of trying to bring as much as I can, I've learned to travel lean.

Once on Jersey, I rented a car and headed straight to Royal Jersey to play that afternoon. On the way to the course, I had one of those funny moments you couldn't plan but become part of the pleasure of traveling. Trying to figure out which road to take, I saw a bumper sticker on the truck in front of me. It read, "*Shit happens, No shit.*" Because I was laughing to myself, I took the wrong road. It cost me 15 minutes, but I laughed the entire time.

The weather couldn't have been better, and I changed into a pair of shorts, something I rarely brought or had a chance to wear in the British Isles. I just so happened to have shorts in my suitcase because of our visit to Italy. I also got a history lesson while on Jersey. During World War II, both Jersey and Guernsey were occupied by Nazi Germany, and during the occupation they built a number of bunkers along the coast in anticipation of an Allied attack. There are several of these bunkers along the first hole at Royal Jersey.

The next morning, I played La Moye Golf Club on the other side of Jersey and near the hotel where I spent the night. La Moye is an excellent course with incredible views of the nearby bay. The following day, I took my first extended ferry ride to the Isle of Guernsey. After my baggage debacle at Gatwick, this mode of transportation was a welcome relief. The weight of my various pieces of luggage was not an issue. Though it wasn't as fast as flying, the ferry was a comfortable and pleasant way to travel. It led me to change my plans. Rather than fly from Guernsey to Gatwick, I decided to take the four-hour ferry ride to the south of England and rent a car at the ferry terminal. It was a smart decision.

I played Royal Guernsey in the afternoon, and of the three Channel Island courses I played, it was my favorite. Though it finished with a par-3, or short hole, it was an excellent 18th hole and the course was—solid start to finish—made better by the remains of old German bunkers and centuries-old fortress remains scattered around the course.

The next day was a long travel day, starting with a ferry ride to Poole. After arriving there, I drove to Southport, England, nearly six hours away. My plan was to play Royal Liverpool, Wallasey, and Southport and Ainsdale before catching a plane to Inverness to meet Buck. The long drive alone gave me time to think, and my thoughts remained on Sally. I wondered where she'd be right now. She would have finished a year at UNCC and would hopefully have been accepted at Carolina for the fall. Would she still be interested in Graeme or found another boy she'd become interested in? As I thought over these things I cried. I missed her so much. While the time I was spending here alone afforded me moments like this, I knew I had a long way to go.

I began this leg of my trip with a round at Royal Liverpool. After finishing and returning to my car, I checked my cell phone and noticed I had a number of missed calls. This shook me and made me assume something bad had happened. I called my secretary, Wanda Baker, who had made a couple of the calls I missed. When I reached her, she asked where I was and was I okay. I told her I was fine and that I was in the western part of England. Then she told me about the London subway bombings and that several people had called to make sure I was safe. I was fine, but listening to the BBC as I drove brought back I had many of the same feelings I'd had on 9/11.

After absorbing the news of the London attacks, I played Southport and Ainsdale in the afternoon. I was disappointed in the opening hole, but beyond that, I thought it was an excellent test and a true links.

The next morning before heading to Manchester for my flight to Inverness, I played Wallasey, which turned out to be my favorite of the three in this segment of my trip. It looked and felt like a true links start to finish. It was also the 16th new course I had played on my trip. At the Manchester airport, security was extremely tight in the aftermath of the London bombings. I expected to pay another big penalty for my luggage but didn't. However, clearing security was far more challenging than before. After arriving in Inverness, I drove to the Morangie House Hotel in Tain, just south of Dornoch. Though the hotel needs a facelift today, it remains one of my favorites. Glenmorangie Scotch Distillery is a stone's throw from the hotel's front door.

Since Buck would not arrive until the next day, I decided to play Brora, where I had not been since playing with a group from Charlotte in 1995. Because I'd been so caught up then with the cows, sheep, and horses around the course, I had little memory of the course itself. This time I focused on it and the layout. While the cows, sheep, and horses still roamed the fairways, I came away with a very positive impression.

That evening after dinner I went to the bar and ordered a double Glenmorangie. The bar was crowded, but I managed to find an empty table in the back. As I enjoyed the single malt, I thought over the last several weeks. It had been a special time. I had played some great new golf courses, and been to Rome, Tuscany, and the Amalfi coast for the first time with Jo and our friends. Memories for a lifetime. Yet, the recognition of what had brought all this to pass was hard not to think about and the heartbreak remained just below the surface. I knew if I continued to think about it, I would start to cry and knew those around me wouldn't understand. I really looked forward to having Buck join me. We had been close friends for nearly 20 years. He has one of the funniest and quickest wits of anybody I'd ever known, so I knew we would not stop laughing the entire time we would be together. I was ready to see him and really appreciative he had wanted to join me.

When Buck arrived, we began our journey down to St. Andrews

for The Open. We played our way around the Dornoch and Moray Firths and then headed to Aberdeen. Along the way, we played Royal Dornoch, Nairn, and Moray Golf Clubs. The morning we were heading to play Cruden Bay, we read a story in the paper where Butch Harmon mentioned that Peterhead Golf Club was a hidden gem. It was only forty-five minutes away, so we decided to go there the following day before driving south to St. Andrews and Greywalls Hotel. For the first six holes, Buck and I wondered why Butch Harmon made note of it. Then we stepped onto the seventh tee and saw before us a great-looking string of holes. This was what Harmon had been talking about. We weren't disappointed.

Buck and me at The 2005 Open

We made our way to The Open Championship, working in rounds as well over the next several days at Muirfield and North Berwick. The Open lacked drama because Tiger was in control from start to finish, much like he had been in 2000. Buck and I flew home on Monday after The Open, and it was hard to imagine a better trip than the one I'd just completed. It was filled with happy memories, and I felt blessed and fortunate to have been able to do it. However, the healing I'd hoped would come while there hadn't happened. My heart still hurt for Sally. I still missed her just as much as I had right after her death.

I knew, though, that my decision to travel to the British Isles was still the right thing to do. Continuing to return to this place I loved, to play the courses that inspired me, remained my best hope for finding peace. As I looked out the window of the plane, I prayed He would grant me what I sought one day. I didn't know if it would happen on my next trip or on a subsequent one, but I had to trust it would come.

As I thought this over, it became clear I could not assume that somewhere along the list of courses from Mr. Steel's book, which I planned to play, I would find it. I decided to add more courses and trust that while there I would find the solace I sought. I made a commitment to myself that if I found it before I'd played all the courses, I might choose not to play anymore. This was not a quest to do something unique or special. It was my sanctuary.

As I did on the flight to Rome, I again pulled out my AA golf book and began going through the book to find more links courses. Given my recognition that not all sources concurred with my definition of a links course, I decided to also include any courses noted as being along the coast of the British Isles. Those were typically noted as cliffside and seaside courses. This would ensure I only played courses I most loved. It's where I felt golf could be played in its purest form. By the time I landed back in the States nearly eight hours later, I had a list of more than 200 courses, and I wasn't finished adding to my list.

23

Accountability - Part Two

~

In the fall, we turned our focus toward building Sally's Y. Earlier in the year the Y conducted a feasibility study that showed overwhelming support for our vision of building a Y near our home in Lincoln County. Given these conclusions and the Cummings' and Keith's humbling show of support, the Charlotte YMCA community embraced and endorsed our plans. They then provided all the help we could ask for. With their decision to allow us to pursue our vision, Mary Tucker, Dean Jones, and Ron Johnston, who worked for the Greater Charlotte Y organization, dedicated themselves to helping us realize our vision. We then toured a number of Charlotte-area YMCAs to look for a prototype for what we hoped to create. We wanted to take pieces we liked from various facilities and incorporate them into what we were designing. The Lowe's YMCA in Mooresville had recently opened and we found it the most appealing. Their goal had been $7 million, and without much analysis on what such a facility would currently cost, we adopted it as our goal. We weren't sure how we were going to get there but we knew we'd find a way. There was an overwhelming sense God would help us find our path. So many things had already happened that told us He and Sally were looking down on us.

Along with me, my brothers Allison and Walter, and our sister Caroline agreed to donate a sizable piece of property near a major intersection under construction off the new four-lane Highway 16 in eastern Lincoln County. Beyond our own pledge, they also made significant financial gifts. The Cummings and the Keiths also made sizable financial donations, reinforcing our conviction that we would make this happen.

I had also recently finished creating the list of courses I wanted to play. It now numbered nearly 300. Again, it was not about accomplishing some bucket list item. It was about trying to find personal closure with what had happened. I had no intention of writing a book or even sharing my story beyond those closest to me, but I did want to keep a personal record of my experience and have it completed by my 60th birthday in 2014. It was and always would be a simple thing—my long walk with Sally.

In early 2006, our legal counsel informed us that the ownership of the bar and their liability insurance carrier were interested in a settlement. We were set to go to trial March 14. Because this was a civil rather than a criminal trial, the only form of punishment would be monetary. As we had previously decided, whatever money Jo and I might receive would go toward the construction of Sally's Y. From the very beginning, once we learned of the gross negligence of the bar that night, this was never about money for us. It was always about holding the responsible parties accountable for their actions. We agreed to meet with representatives of the company, but we had no interest in any settlement that would stop short of putting them out of business.

Under North Carolina General Statue 18B-305(a), commonly referred to as the Dram Shop Law, it is unlawful to knowingly sell alcohol to an intoxicated person. Under this law, when a permit to open a bar is issued, this responsibility and obligation goes beyond the holder of that permit, and they must ensure that their employees understand their responsibility, duties, and the serious nature of serving someone they know or should know is intoxicated. Based on what we learned through legal discovery, the server for Shimp and his friends had not been trained or instructed in how to handle a patron they believed was intoxicated.

Still, even without such guidance, how could someone not expect a person who is served six pints of beer and three shooters in an hour-and-a-half to be intoxicated? When does a person's sense of responsibility kick in?

Based on what we were told, we also believe one of the bar's owners was behind the bar that night. Hearing this, I was even more determined to take them down and leave them with nothing. Not only had they failed in their responsibility to adequately train the person who served Shimp, they had played a direct role in taking Sally and Grace from us while ruining the lives of Suzanne Kessler and Shimp in the process. I could see no justification for allowing the bar to stay in business. I was prepared to chase them to the end of the earth to make this happen.

All families involved rejected the settlement offer, and our counsel then convened a meeting to discuss our next steps. We were told that bar owners, like many others, create what amounts to a shell game in how they hide their own assets and protect other interests from attack. Our counsel told us that while this could eventually be unraveled they were not prepared to pursue it, given the amount of time it would take and what they might find. We were told to expect only the exhaustion of the full face amount of the liability insurance associated with this location. They advised us that the bar had recently closed, and while they were confident of winning a significant judgment and obtaining punitive damages, their recommendation was to demand the full amount of the policy and agree to settle without going to court.

It was difficult to hear and more difficult to accept. No one wanted to let up, believing we would prevail in the end. However, a sense of weariness and the recognition of an emotionally difficult trial convinced us to think about a settlement. After a week, Jo, Anne, Dick, and I agreed that any offer of less than full face value of the insurance policy was unacceptable. We would reject it and go to trial. We also asked that the ownership acknowledge fault in court. If they chose not to acknowledge their complicity in the accident, we would still accept the settlement, believing the payout acknowledged the bar's role in taking Sally and Grace from us.

As the trial date approached, the bar owners and insurance company continued to offer less than the full amount and we were prepared to go to court. Privately, I hoped they wouldn't meet our demands. Though I never told anyone, I wanted to get them into a courtroom. Their resistance only added to my anger and determination. I wanted to take them down to the fullest extent possible.

One day before the trial was scheduled to begin, they accepted our settlement demand, but they would not openly acknowledge fault in court. At the hearing the next day, the attorneys told the judge a settlement had been reached. After the judge accepted the settlement, I asked permission to read a statement on behalf of our two families. As I read the statement, tears flowed.

"There is no joy or happiness in the outcome of today's hearing. While we take comfort in knowing we have ensured all those responsible for this senseless and heartbreaking tragedy have been held accountable, our lives will never be the same. Never again in this life will I see Sally's beautiful smile, share with her our mutual love of Carolina basketball, or attend a country music concert with her and Grace, or

hear Grace's voice call "Uncle David." Sally was a ray of sunshine in a dark room and together these girls were our families' sunshine. Their absence will always be felt.

"It remains incomprehensible to me how a sober, responsible person or persons would think that after serving someone six pints of beer and three shots of liquor in little more than an hour-and-a-half's time, they could drive a car. Heartbreakingly, their failure and negligence to do so contributed to taking from us the most precious gift God gives us and that is a child. By today's outcome, we hope to send a very loud and clear message to all restaurants and bars who serve alcohol. If you fail to take seriously your obligation to serve your patrons in a responsible manner, you run the risk of being held accountable should they leave your place of business and negligently and recklessly operate their vehicle. On this evening, you loaded the gun. Mr. Shimp simply pulled the trigger."

With Shimp's guilty plea to two counts of second-degree murder and now the bar ownership's acknowledgment of fault by paying monetary damages and shutting down the bar, I felt we had done all we could to hold accountable those most responsible for this nightmare. We did it not just for our own sense of justice; we did it for Sally and Grace. We had to do it for them.

The settlement provided some sense of closure. Still, it didn't make me miss Sally any less or provide a way to move on. I could only hope that I might find a way to do so on one of the golf courses on my list one day in the future.

24

Wales: A True Hidden Gem

~

Of the countries that comprise the British Isles, I was least familiar with Wales. Other than being the homeland of Tom Jones, the pop singer from the 1970s, I knew little about it and even less about its golf courses. Donald Steel's book included seven courses in Wales, but as far as I knew, Royal Porthcawl was the only one worth recognition. Over two weeks in June, I quickly learned how much I didn't know.

Using three sources—the AA book, Mr. Steel's book, and a book published by the Sunday Telegraph that I later learned Mr. Steel helped to publish while working there—I found 19 courses that qualified as links, cliffside, or seaside layouts. I put together an itinerary that started in northern Wales and allowed me to play my way around the coast to the south. I could play all the courses on my new list in Wales on this trip.

Before leaving, I taped my favorite photograph of Sally and Grace inside the side pocket of my golf bag. It was the picture I took at Sea Island in 2003. I also included a portfolio of other pictures I had of the girls, along with ones of Jo, Reynolds, and

Graham to carry with me. After arriving in Manchester on June 4, I headed off to the Bodysgallen Hotel, where I planned to stay for four nights. The key word here is "planned." As happened fairly often on future trips, I would change my itinerary for a number of reasons. Rarely did a trip go exactly as I'd planned.

This time, I began making changes quickly. After finishing my first round at North Wales Golf Club and while enjoying a Tennant's lager in their bar, I noticed a publication on a table touting Wales and the 2010 Ryder Cup matches to be played at Celtic Manor. Curiosity got the best of me, and I leafed through the publication, which included an extensive list of the various courses in Wales. I noticed several courses that seemed to belong on my list but weren't there. They were Bull Bay, Porthmadog, Nefyn and District, and St. David's City, a nine-hole course. It was the picture of Nefyn and District that got my attention. It appeared to be situated on a spectacular site like Old Head in Ireland.

This discovery presented me with a dilemma. The list of courses I had originally decided to play was only in Donald Steel's book. With my decision the previous summer to use other resources to add all courses situated around the coasts of the British Isles that were described as links, seaside, or clifftop, I had to consider that beyond these, I might find out about other courses from other resources. I also had to acknowledge that some I originally added might not, after further information, actually be a course along the immediate coast of the Isles. I felt I needed then to decide how I would handle this.

I had another pint of Tennant's to help me decide. After much thought, it was clear to me that if I intended to make my list complete, I had to allow for changes, especially courses I discovered at the last minute that met my various classifications. It was also okay to strike courses if I got there and realized they didn't really fit where I wanted to play. I then revised my itinerary so I could play all the courses I wanted to play while in Wales, including the ones I had just discovered. As I would come to learn, I could often show up at a club as a single, ask if there was room for me that day, and almost always get to play.

After falling asleep that night, something I will never forget happened. While sleeping, I became aware of someone first sitting, then lying down next to me on the bed. Sensing their presence, I immediately sat up and turned on the bedside light. No one was there. I checked the door. It was still locked. I checked the window, and it was slightly cracked, just the way I had left it. I don't know if it was Sally, but I have no doubt that someone got beside me on the bed that night.

The next day I played three courses including Conwy. Of the courses I played while in the northern part of Wales, it was my favorite. It looked and played like a true links, which had earned its mention in Steel's book. North Wales was a close second, another true links with adjacent par-3s—the 16th and 17th—that criss-cross among a series of dunes, an excellent pair of holes.

As for Bull Bay and Llandudno Maesdu, while both are good courses, they represented a perfect example of the challenge of my list and the difficulty in classifying courses. Maesdu, while having some links elements, looked and played much more like a parkland course, so much so that I probably would not have it on my list in hindsight. Bull Bay was a combination of clifftop and heathland, and that affirmed my decision to play it.

After playing Bull Bay, I headed to the Seiont Manor hotel for several nights with Holyhead and Anglesey on my agenda for the next day. While playing Holyhead, I noticed a sign next to a tee. The sign read, "In order not to offend local residents, please do not use this as a toilet."

I couldn't help but laugh, because I knew exactly why it had been placed there. It also got me thinking about how often signs are used around golf courses in the British Isles to get a point or message across. They use them far more often than we do in the U.S. Many have hilarious messages, whether intentional or in the context in which they are placed. Given this, I decided to begin keeping a photographic collection of my favorites.

Over the next few days I played some of the finest links and clifftop courses anywhere. I could not have been more wrong to have thought that Royal Porthcawl was the only course in Wales worthy of recognition. In fact, Wales is the hidden gem among the British Isles.

For true links courses, in addition to Conwy, North Wales, and Royal Porthcawl, there are not many better in the British Isles than Royal St. Davids, Aberdovey, Borth and Ynyslas, Ashburnham, Tenby, Pennard, and Pyle and Kenfig.

For clifftop courses, Neyfn and District proved to be the hidden gem within the hidden gem. The setting was indeed spectacular and the golf was excellent as well. The day I played could not have been better. The temperature was mild and the wind light. It was beautiful and the blue water in Caernarfon Bay sparkled. As I made my way around the course and took in God's work where this course had been placed, thoughts of Sally became overwhelming. As happened often, I began to talk to her as I played. While knowing she was there in spirit, I would have loved to share the view that I was fortunate enough to see with her and also Jo. As I played the back nine of the Old Course that is routed across a narrow peninsula, I was awestruck. God had indeed put a golf course here, and fortunately it had been discovered. It was natural and rugged but truly special. I was glad I amended my trip to include it, reinforcing my decision to be open to adding more courses should I hear of ones that fit. The timing of finding that magazine was profound.

When I reached the tee of the 14th hole, a downhill par-3 that is situated on a concrete platform almost at the very end of the peninsula, I walked to the back of the platform as I looked out to the sea and cried. There was no one behind me, so I pulled the portfolio of pictures out of my bag and took a seat for a few minutes while I looked through it. It was a moment of reflection and the "what ifs." Finally, before playing the hole, I pulled one of the balls out of my pocket with the sunflower and "My Sweet Sally" on it and hit it off the back of the tee into Caernarfon Bay. This was something I would often do on future courses, leaving a little bit of Sally there when I found myself standing on a beautiful part of God's creation.

In addition to Neyfn, Southerndown is another outstanding clifftop course. Some of the views from the course are similarly special and the golf is also excellent. The 18th hole, with a two-tiered fairway, was my favorite and reminded me of some of Nicklaus's designs.

Over my days in Wales, several noteworthy things happened that again challenged my list of courses. One day I had planned to play Aberdovey in the morning, Cardigan in the afternoon, and finish at St. Davids City, one of the courses I added to my list at North Wales. It was an ambitious bit of scheduling that included a challenging drive, but I felt I could get it all in since St. David's City was a nine-hole course. After finishing my rounds at Aberdovey and Cardigan, it was already past five. I had about an hour drive to St. David's. Beyond that, I still had a two-and-a-half-hour drive back to my hotel.

As I started toward St. David's, I considered what time I would finish. The thought of facing such a long drive back made me wonder if I really had to play this course. I was hungry, and a glass of wine would taste great after the 36 holes I'd already played. I contemplated that since I had just added St. David's to my list, maybe it didn't need to be included. When I reached the point in the road where I could go right to play golf or left to my hotel, I turned left. I chose food and wine.

It wasn't the only time I amended my golf schedule. When I played Pyle and Kenfig, a competition was underway. I had to wait nearly two hours before teeing off. After playing several holes, I found myself on the wrong hole and had no idea where I'd gotten turned around. Instead of a lost golf ball, I was a lost golfer. I wound up in the middle of the competition, which further frustrated me. As I considered my options, I decided that since I'd at least played a few holes, it would count as having played Pyle and

Kenfig, so I headed back to my car. My conscience, however, soon kicked in and both decisions began to haunt me. While accepting that whatever list I developed was only that, my list, I needed to remain constant in where I proposed to play and how I approached each round.

Playing Tenby, I again found myself behind a competition. With no chance of playing through, I began hitting multiple shots on each hole to keep from getting bored. A threesome was playing directly in front of me, and though I never hit into them, they continually looked back in my direction. After several holes, they waved for me to play up, and I wasn't sure what to expect when I reached them. To my surprise, they asked me to join them, even though they were playing a competition. I accepted their kind offer.

I told them I was from the U.S., and, after finishing, they asked why I was there and playing alone. With much reluctance, I told them about Sally and Grace and showed them some pictures from the portfolio. As I showed the pictures, the tears began again. They insisted I join them for a lager. While in the bar, I learned that one was the club captain and another was the club secretary. They were eager to know my opinion of Tenby and the other courses I'd played in Wales.

Unlike many clubs in Scotland, Ireland, and parts of England, their club, like most in Wales, rarely got visitor play, especially from Americans. Visitor play is a huge source of income for many clubs in the British Isles, and they asked me what they could do to attract more outside play to their clubs. I told them the courses I'd played along the coast were every bit as good as those I'd played in Scotland, Ireland, or England. The challenge was logistics. Most Americans spend about a week on their golf trips and they're most familiar with the courses they've seen on television or those they've read about in magazine travel stories. I shared with them the magazine I'd come across in North Wales and said it was a great way to promote golf in their country. With the Ryder Cup headed to Celtic Manor in four years, golf in Wales would benefit greatly from the international exposure that would come. I told them I'd sing its praises, feeling strongly that golf in Wales was deserving of the time and effort to get there, where others could discover what I had—extraordinary golf. They were appreciative of my thoughts on the matter and offered again their condolences for such a heartbreaking loss.

The last course I played in Wales was Royal Porthcawl, and it lived up to its reputation. Even after playing all these courses, it was my favorite course in Wales, with several others a close second. I felt enlightened, having discovered the depth and quality of golf in Wales that I'd never known existed.

Though I'd added courses to my itinerary, my pace of play left me with three open days before my flight home. It gave me time to drive south into western England to play Saunton East and West, Royal North Devon (more commonly known as Westward Ho!), and St. Enedoc before heading back to the U.S. At Royal North Devon, like Brora, I found myself playing among cows and horses and it would not be the last time I ran across livestock on the golf course or more amusing signs.

Flying home, I reflected on whether I was any closer to finding peace about Sally. Tears, once so elusive, now were a frequent companion, as had been the case at Nefyn and District. I knew there was still a long walk ahead of me before I would find it.

One of my long-held dreams was to attend a Ryder Cup, and with the next one scheduled to be played at the K Club in Ireland that fall, I suggested to Jo when I got home from Wales that we make the trip if we could get tickets and a place to stay at a reasonable price. I contacted Adventures in Golf, a travel agency I'd read about, and one of the owners, Carl Johnson, helped us secure tickets and a place to stay.

In addition to attending the Ryder Cup, we also arranged to play several courses on my list, including The European Club. After our round there, Pat Ruddy, who designed, built, and still owned the course, was in the clubhouse. Before taking up golf course design and ownership, he had been a golf writer. He also designed several other courses in Ireland that were on my list. Seeing us in the bar, he came over and introduced himself. He asked what we thought of The European Club and where else we had played on our trip. I was often asked this same question. With reluctance, I shared our story and he was genuinely touched. He said he'd never considered playing such a list of courses, but it was something he would give some thought to in the future. Before leaving, we asked for a photo with him.

I'm glad to say I've been to a Ryder Cup, but it's not a spectator-friendly event. There is so little golf actually being played and so many people there to watch. The best you can do is catch small glimpses of the action, which is limited to a handful of groups each day. In my opinion, the best way to see the Ryder Cup is from a comfortable chair in front of a television.

In Memory Of One—A Vision For All

25

2007: A Year
of Significance

Over the course of 2006, our efforts to see Sally's Y become reality continued. After receiving the go ahead from the Y to begin our capital campaign, Jo and I focused our full attention on doing just that. Beyond the initial group that pledged their support, many others agreed to help. We were humbled by the outpouring of support we received, and it continued to speak to Sally's beautiful legacy and the impact of her life on so many.

The Y also engaged the firm, Red Moon Marketing, to help us put together material that would be needed for our capital campaign effort. The company did an incredible job. The people there developed a logo specifically for Sally's Y and a slogan that carried significant meaning: "In Memory of One, A Vision for All." By the end of 2006, we were close to $4 million in pledges and actual donations. There was no doubt we would eventually reach our goal. God and Sally were blessing our efforts.

Given the progress we were making, Johnny and Deborah Harris and Steve and Karen Cummings agreed to hold a fundraiser for Sally's Y at Quail Hollow in March 2007, with the hope that it would provide another major boost toward our goal. Earlier in the year, our efforts received a tremendous lift when the area's largest hospital and healthcare provider, Carolinas Healthcare, came to our family about purchasing property next to where we planned to locate Sally's Y. They wanted to move forward with development of the site as soon as possible, as they had been granted a certificate of need for a same-day surgery center in East Lincoln. Based on the development plans, we agreed to donate over 20 acres next to the hospital for the Y and also donate another 85 acres to Catawba Lands Conservancy that the Y would be able to use for recreational purposes. The combination of the two made for a unique partnership that to the best of everyone's knowledge does not exist anywhere else in the country.

As part of the fundraiser, Jo and I were asked to tape a video to be played at the beginning of the program. We were to talk about Sally and our decision to honor her memory by building a YMCA that would be named for her. The previous year, we had been asked to do something similar for Greater Charlotte YMCA's annual banquet, and it was almost too much for me. They had to stop taping a number of times so I could regroup. I don't know how that video turned out, because I couldn't find the strength to go and risk breaking down in front of the hundreds of people surrounding me.

Prior to taping this second video, I vowed to do my best, but I told everyone how difficult it would be for me. They also asked for a couple of songs that captured the essence of Sally and our efforts. I suggested to Jo that "I Can Only Imagine" by Jeff Carson, "I Believe" by Diamond Rio, or "One Sweet Day" by Mariah Carey accompanied by Boyz II Men might fit. We worried that none of the songs fit Sally or the moment just right but felt that "I Can Only Imagine" probably came closest.

At the taping, I went first, while Jo waited nearby with Mary

Tucker and Lauren Byrne from Red Moon. I held it together better than in my previous effort to tape a message, but it was still a struggle. Taping had to be stopped a number of times. When I went back to where Jo, Mary, and Lauren were waiting, all three were in tears. Jo asked me to listen to a song Lauren had found, written and performed by Jo Dee Messina, called "Heaven Was Needing a Hero." Listening to it, I could barely breathe as my emotions welled up inside me. The title said so much. When Lauren played the song, I cried with each verse and knew it was the song we wanted. It captured everything imaginable about Sally. God needed a hero and chose Sally. The verse that hit me the hardest was, "If I knew the last time that I held you was the last time, I'd never let go." I thought again of why I hadn't told her to stay where she was that night or why I hadn't gone to pick them up.

Through the efforts of Johnny, Deborah, Steve, and Karen, we had a great event at Quail Hollow on March 27. I had been asked to introduce the video. When it came time for me to speak, I knew I couldn't. The song was too much. Steve saw it in my face and told me he'd handle the introduction. I headed out of the room. I didn't want to detract from what was being done on our behalf, but I couldn't be in there. Greg saw me slip out and followed me, putting his arm around me in the hallway while I fell apart. The event was a tremendous success and by early summer, we had more than $5.5 million in pledges.

In late May, I headed back to Scotland and Ireland to continue playing courses on my list. It was the first of three trips there during the year. For the first time, I brought a Garmin GPS unit with me, and I mounted it on the windshield of my rental car after arriving in Glasgow. I pre-loaded the unit with maps for the UK before I left, hoping it would make traveling easier and faster. My usual strategy had been to study a map the night before I was going to play, make notes about key roads and towns on my route, and lay the papers on the passenger seat, where they'd be easy for me to see. Although they do a very good job of marking their roads to help get you where you're going, it can still be a challenge navigating the narrow roads and roundabouts throughout the British Isles. It was time, I'd decided, to introduce technology to my travels.

If it were only that easy. As I made my way out of the airport, I came upon a series of roundabouts, and a woman's voice with an English accent began giving me directions faster than I could process them. I was immediately confused and was soon headed north rather than my intended direction of south—and the voice didn't help. She kept offering ways to correct my path but I couldn't focus. I finally had to pull off the road and regroup. That meant yanking the GPS unit off the dash and throwing it on the floor. I then pulled out a map and went back to plotting my drive the good old-fashioned way.

It would be years before I would try a navigation system again in the British Isles, and I only did it then because Jo got us lost reading a map and we needed GPS to get us back to our hotel. Fortunately, the all-knowing voice was more deliberate and patient that time. Just in case, I still keep a map with me when I'm there.

Between the jet lag, my frustrating episode with the GPS, and a three-hour drive, I have little recollection about Silloth on Solway, the course I was headed to play. By the time I finished playing, all I wanted to do was get to my hotel and go to bed, but a two-hour drive still faced me. As I headed back toward Scotland, I was a few miles down the road when I heard a strange sound on the roof of my car. I wasn't sure what it was, but I continued to drive. Then it hit me. Where was my Nikon E8700 camera? I pulled off the road and searched the interior of the car. It wasn't there. I checked my golf bag in the trunk. It wasn't there, either. I realized that the sound I'd heard must have been my camera falling off the car. I drove back to where I'd heard the sound and found my camera—in about three pieces. I felt sick. I had fortunately brought another camera with me, but the E8700 was my favorite. It was easy to carry in my golf bag and, while it was primarily a point and shoot camera, it had several nice features that provided some control of the image.

I picked up what was left of it and continued my drive to the southern part of Scotland to play five courses around Dumfries and Galloway over the next several days. From there, I took the ferry from Portpatrick to Belfast. I then headed north to play my way through Northern Ireland and then along the northern coast of Ireland down to Shannon Airport, from where I would fly home.

While on this particular trip, I began to consider for the first time the possibility of creating a journal or record of my walk that I might be willing to share with others. It had always been in my mind from the beginning to create something for myself that I could look through, as I did with the other books and the photo albums from earlier trips I took with me to Quail. However, as more friends and acquaintances heard about what I hoped to do, they asked for a copy of whatever I might put together. Many encouraged me to write a book.

Truthfully, I wondered if I'd play all the courses on my list. The primary reason I was here was to grieve on my own and hope somewhere along the way I came to terms with losing Sally. If that happened before I finished, I might not come back and continue playing the courses on my list. If I committed to a book, this might add pressure I didn't want. Also, I felt wholly inadequate to write a book, so I set that idea aside for the time being. On June 13, I headed to Achill Island to play the nine-hole course there.

It was a day earlier than I had planned, but I felt I'd have no problem getting on the course. It was the middle of the week and not a place where someone needed to arrange tee times in advance. As luck would have it, they were holding an open competition for ladies beginners and they were just about to begin when I arrived. If I hurried, I hoped I could start and be out of their way before the competition began. It seemed simple enough—to me anyway.

Because a competition was being held, a lady was there to collect the money from the competitors. She noticed me pulling my clubs from my car. Upon walking up, I asked her if I could go out first, but she told me that would be impossible. There was a competition about to get underway and the first tee was booked. No outside play would be allowed until the competition had ended. In my travels here to play golf, I had learned you don't mess with competitions, particularly involving ladies. I could write another book about that.

I told the lady I had driven two-and-a-half hours to play and hoped she might find a way to accommodate me. After much consultation with other ladies, she agreed to let me tee off after the final group had teed off. That meant waiting two hours in my car, since the clubhouse was closed. I did it. I sat in my car waiting for all the ladies to tee off, knowing the nine holes I was about to play might be the longest nine holes I'd ever play. I turned out to be right. I'd hit one shot, then wait about fifteen minutes to hit the next one.

To entertain myself between shots, I began taking selfies using the self-timer on my camera. It would become a favorite pastime on future trips when I encountered long waits. Sitting on a bench while doing this, an idea came to me about sharing my story with others. Though I didn't know them personally, I had always thought highly of Ron Green, Sr. and Ron Green, Jr., who wrote about golf for the *Charlotte Observer*. Both were incredibly gifted writers who had a special way to communicate the basis of their story with a wonderful sense of humor and wit. I decided when I got back to my hotel Stella Maris, I would email Ron, Jr. to see if he would be willing to meet with me to help figure out how to put something together. If he declined, I would understand and I'd come up with another approach if I still had thoughts of sharing my journey with others.

The selfie the *Charlotte Observer* used

I sent Ron, Jr. an email the next morning, and when I returned from golf, he had responded and offered to meet with me in late July. It was the first of many times when something happened that told me the idea of writing a book was the right thing to do. It felt as if it was something God expected me to do, and Ron seemed to be the right person to talk with about my idea. I feel very fortunate and blessed that he agreed to talk with me.

As my trip came to a close, my last round was again to play Lahinch. While overcast and cool like it had been in 2004, the wind was much calmer. As I stood on the first tee holding one of my logo balls and waiting for the starter to allow me to tee off, I reflected on all that had taken place since that day when I stood here with my life in absolute turmoil, holding that special ball that came to signify and mean so much to me when I finished. It was with me again, but this time in the top pocket of my golf bag where it would always remain. As I stood with tears welling in my eyes, all I could do was close them and shake my head at all that had happened since that round. We had held accountable those most responsible for taking Sally and Grace from us, and we were now making great progress to build Sally's Y. With these accomplishments, I could feel a sense of closure and relief. Yet, the tears and the well of emotion inside told me I still had much further to go to find that inner peace I decided to seek here that day in 2004.

As I made my way around the course, I remembered certain moments when I thought I'd lost the ball. After playing the sixth and walking over the seventh tee, I walked to the back of the tee and hit one of my logo balls in Liscannor Bay. It was okay now to lose a ball, and I left a little bit of Sally there.

That night I stayed at the Moy House just outside of town. It would become a favorite for me and eventually also for Jo. As I sat in their main living area enjoying a whiskey—this time rather than

Glenmorangie, the Irish equivalent Bushmills—I sat looking out the window. It was still light, and I reflected on what had again been an incredible trip. Since I'd left, I had played in England, Scotland, Northern Ireland, and the Republic of Ireland. I had managed to play 38 different courses, 34 of them new to me. On multiple days I played 54 holes. I was now physically exhausted, and based on how my clothes fit, I had lost weight. Emotionally, while what had happened earlier in the day told me I had much further to go on my walk to find peace with losing Sally, I missed Jo, Reynolds, and Graham and was ready to get home to see them. They were my reason for living.

In July, I headed back to Scotland but with Jo, Reynolds, and Graham in what we thought might be our final family trip. Reynolds had continued to date Jennifer Tingen, the girl he'd gone out with for the first time on the night of Sally's accident. Reynolds had let us know he wanted to ask her to marry him by the end of the year. We also took Anne, Katie, and Christopher with us, while Graham invited his closest friend, Lee Cummings, to join us.

We flew into Inverness and spent several nights at Tulchan. We made another trip to Royal Dornoch, taking Katie and Christopher with us, while the boys tried their luck salmon fishing in the River Spey. Anne spent her time sightseeing, and then we all headed south to stay in the Colonel's house at Greywalls. From there, we could go watch The Open Championship at Carnoustie. We also made a side trip to play North Berwick with Katie and Christopher.

I still smile at the memories of our trip. It was our first extended family trip since the accident, and it was everything we hoped it would be. More than once, we found ourselves crying when a memory of Sally and Grace came up, knowing how much they would have enjoyed being there with us. Flying home, I asked Jo if could return in October to continue playing courses on my list.

After returning home, I put together a trip that would center on the southwest corner of Scotland. I had purchased a newer edition of the AA's golf guide, and it included more information about the courses I wanted to play, including websites and email addresses that helped me plan my trip. As I reviewed the information it provided, I realized it was now possible to handle all the arrangements for my trips myself and I wouldn't need help from a travel agent.

On August 7, I met Ron at Quail Hollow, and over lunch I shared with him some of the details about what I was doing. I mentioned the growing number of requests I'd received for a copy of whatever record I might create of my journey and asked if he'd be willing to help. Ron told me he'd give it some thought and get back to me in a few weeks. I honestly think he wasn't sure what to make of what I shared and needed to check with others to be sure it was true.

A week later he contacted me and asked if I would be willing to allow him to write an article for the *Charlotte Observer*. I'd never thought about that, and this time I asked him for some time to think about it. After talking with Jo, I decided if there were anyone

I could trust to write something so personal and private in a broad publication, Ron would be the one. I have never regretted my decision.

At Quail Hollow in late August, another longtime personal friend, Mac Everett, expressed his desire to go with me on one of my trips. I was surprised. Mac is one of the greatest guys I've had the pleasure to know, but I knew he stayed very busy and thought he was just trying to be supportive. I told Mac I'd let him know when I began to put a trip together for the following year, fully expecting him to tell me the dates wouldn't work. I would be wrong.

In early October, I flew back into Glasgow—this time I handled the airport roundabouts without a GPS—and headed south for nine days. I played all the courses I had not played in North and South Ayrshire as well as on Arran. I also made return visits to Turnberry Ailsa, Royal Troon, Western Gailes, and Prestwick. I played Turnberry Kintyre as well, which had been called the Arran course on my first visit in 1986 but had since been redesigned with several new holes added.

This was the first and only trip when I became concerned about my safety. I had played 45 holes one day and wanted to get in 18 more before calling it a day. I headed to a municipal course in Troon that bordered what appeared to be public housing. Making the turn far from the clubhouse, I saw three teenagers following me. The course was virtually empty except for two groups of men a couple of holes ahead of me. As I was about to hit a shot, the boys approached me. They asked where I was from, and when I told them I was from the U.S., they laughed and walked away. They continued to stay behind me, and with a sense of concern, I pulled out my 5-iron and carried it in one hand. I had closed in on the group of men playing in front of me, and I was relieved when they motioned for me to play up. The boys disappeared and I breathed a sigh of relief. The men were on holiday from Sweden and could not have been nicer. They spoke fluent English. They had seen the boys following me and sensed I was in trouble. I played the final holes with them as the sun set on a long day.

When I returned home, I called Mac to tell him about my plans for my next trip. To my surprise, he said he would love to join me and would clear his calendar to make it possible.

Our capital campaign for Sally's Y had continued to go well with pledges in excess of $6 million by the end of the year, including a generous donation from Jimmie and Chani Johnson. Dianne also wanted to honor Randy and took a significant naming opportunity. We were humbled and grateful to them both, along with many others, for the continued outpouring of support for our vision to honor Sally's memory. So many people were doing so much.

Unfortunately, at the same time, the economy was beginning to crash. Lehman Brothers would file for bankruptcy in August. With Charlotte's economy driven by Wachovia and Bank of America's presence and the exponential growth in real estate development and values, the implications for Charlotte's future, should the economy worsen, worried everyone and raised questions about our ability to complete our capital campaign. Still, we had faith we would get it done.

Reynolds and Jennifer were engaged at Christmas and set a wedding date in October 2008. I was reminded of Reverend Lisa Saunders' offer to pray that one day we would be blessed with a granddaughter.

26

Big Events

~⌣~

Ron's story about me was published in late January in the *Charlotte Observer*, and my trust in him to properly tell a difficult, emotional, and personal story was more than affirmed. I felt tremendous emotion reading what he'd written about all we had discussed over a series of lunches since our first meeting the previous August. The story also included two pictures that added to what he wrote. Prior to the story being published, Ron had asked if the *Observer* could shoot some photos of me at Quail Hollow. I was uncomfortable with the idea but agreed to do it, trusting his control over the story. The photographer took at least one hundred pictures. Ron also asked if I could send some of my own photographs from my travels, and I sent more than fifty. He also wanted the *Observer* to take some pictures at our home. I reluctantly agreed.

When I opened the Sunday paper with the story about me, I saw they had chosen a self-portrait I had taken at Achill Island when I first had the thought to contact Ron. It overwhelmed me with emotion thinking about the symmetry, a feeling I shared in an email to Ron. The other photograph was one taken at our home that included my bracelet, one of my logo golf balls, and a picture of Sally and Grace. I'm thankful to this day for the sensitivity Ron showed in writing this story. The only possible downside was that even more people asked me to chronicle my story. I knew at some point I'd at least have to try to do it—hopefully, though, with Ron's help.

With all the progress we'd made in 2007 toward our goal for Sally's Y, we felt it was time to hold a special event at Quail Hollow, including a golf outing at Ballantyne Country Club, to complete our fundraising. Many friends volunteered to help and we began organizing the event in March with an October 16 event date. It would be a busy October with Reynolds and Jennifer getting married on October 4. I couldn't help but think about how life works sometimes. In a two-week period, we hoped to finish our effort to honor Sally's memory and also welcome a new daughter-in-law to our family.

We struggled to find an appropriate theme for the fundraiser, and while driving one day, I had a thought. Sally loved country music, and Paul Schadt was her favorite DJ. I called Clear Channel in Charlotte and, after talking with a receptionist, I was connected to general manager Morgan Bohannan. I told him what we were doing and why I was calling. He promised to speak with Paul about it and fully expected him to say yes. A few hours later, Morgan called back to tell me that Paul would be honored to emcee the event. I was in awe at how things were coming together. I called Mary Tucker to share the news with our committee, and we chose a theme based on country music. The next challenge for the organizing committee was finding a band or musician for the evening.

Several days later, as I thought about whom we could get, I suddenly thought of Jo Dee Messina and what it would mean to have her there to perform "Heaven Was Needing a Hero." She was among Sally's favorite artists. I wasn't sure how to go about contacting her or whether she would have any interest. I only knew I had to try. At our next committee meeting, I told Jo and everyone else what I hoped to do, asking if they agreed and what we could pay her to perform. Everyone liked the idea but doubted we could pay her what she would require. I decided to again call Morgan to get Jo Dee Messina's agent's number. Morgan offered to make the call himself.

We didn't get an answer for several weeks, but as happened so many times, it felt as if God and Sally's hands were touching what we were doing. Morgan called to tell me that Jo Dee had told her agent she wanted to be part of our event with one condition—beyond a nominal payment, a member of her band wanted to play golf at Quail Hollow. That was easy enough to arrange. I would have hosted the entire band if they wanted to play.

In late May, Mac and I were off to England and Scotland for a week-and-a-half. I arrived a couple of days before Mac, and we connected on the Isle of Mann to play Castletown and Rowany Golf Club.

Hitting a shot at Castletown that Mac took. A favorite.

It was a truly memorable trip for us both, filled with so many special moments. I especially appreciated his interest in joining me. I took Mac to some places he would not have otherwise ever played or even thought of playing, and at times the look on his face was priceless. I managed to catch it with a photograph one time as two sheep were baying when we headed out to play.

It was pouring rain on the day we went to play Furness Golf Club. Furness is also a course few, if any, Americans would ever consider playing. It is well off the beaten path. When we arrived at the club, there was only one car in the parking lot. We found the clubhouse open but couldn't locate anyone. We finally came across a gentleman in the locker room and told him, despite the conditions, that we'd like to play. He introduced himself as the club secretary and asked us to follow him to his office. It was clear to us that he didn't know quite what to make of us showing up there on such a rainy day with our American accent.

As we entered his office, he took a seat behind his desk. He then looked up and asked, "Are you sure you're at the right club?" Mac and I broke out laughing and said we were and we indeed wanted to play. This type of exchange was new to Mac, but it wasn't the first nor the last time I'd get a quizzical look from the locals when I showed up to play.

In addition to the more obscure courses we played, Mac and I also teed it up at Royal Birkdale and Royal Lytham and St. Annes. The Open Championship was set for Birkdale that year and guest play had been limited during the time we were visiting. I'd made several attempts to secure us a tee time but hadn't had any success. I was sure we'd struck out. However, during the Wachovia Championship, Mac spoke with Ian Baker-Finch, who was there with CBS Sports, about our trip and asked if he could help us get on at Birkdale where Baker-Finch had won the 1991 Open Championship. Ian made a phone call. Following his appearance in the 1997 Open at Royal Troon, Ian had given up playing professional golf. He is now one of the most respected individuals in golf and is revered at Royal Birkdale. His call secured our play, but we were told that we would need to play with members. Given that the request came from Ian, we were paired with the club's current president and a past captain.

Among the surprises of the trip was St. Annes Old Links Golf Club, adjacent to Royal Lytham. We were both impressed by the course, an outstanding links that we would recommend to anyone playing golf in the Merseyside area of England.

After finishing a round, Mac and I usually headed to the clubhouse bar for lunch to have a sandwich, which was often a BLT or their version of a club sandwich. I'd regularly order a side of chips (what we call French fries) and a lager. Invariably, someone would determine we were from the States from our accent or dress and come by to ask what we thought of their course, where we had played previously, and where we were headed from there. After praising their course and telling them where we were playing next, they would almost always say, "Well, you need to play Silloth on Solway." We heard it so much that Mac and I started laughing about it and decided we needed to work it into our trip, even though I'd played it a year earlier. At least we'd be able to tell the next person who recommended it that we were on our way.

The day we got to Silloth on Solway, the wind blew close to 40 miles per hour and it took everything we had just to finish 18 holes. When we were done, we settled into the bar and saw a foursome of Americans on the first tee. About that time, the rain came gushing down and two of the guys we were watching tried to use their umbrellas. Big mistake in 40-mile-per-hour wind.

Over the course of this trip I played 31 courses. When I got home, plans were well underway for the event at Quail in October, with friends and businesses graciously offering donations and underwriting the event. Additional pledges had been received over the first half of the year, and we were optimistic that we could cap the celebration by announcing we had reached our goal and construction would soon begin. However, the economy continued to falter. The financial industry, real estate, and the stock market were taking a beating. In hopes of raising what we needed, I suggested raffling off a Mini Cooper. Hendrick Mini agreed to sell us one just above cost and would wait for payment until after the raffle. We chose a yellow-and-black model, because it reminded everyone of the sunflowers Sally loved so much. We also planned to put sunflowers on the tables at the event and name the tables for country music artists. It was going to be a special event.

In late September, Wachovia went under and the implications for Charlotte were enormous. It also raised questions about the potential success of our event. We hoped for 350 guests, but we were still well below that number of commitments.

On October 4, Reynolds and Jennifer were married, and although it was a special day for our family, Sally's absence was impossible to ignore. Weddings had been difficult for Jo and me to attend, particularly for me.

Jo had recently found the strength to attend weddings and attended some of Sally's friends, but I chose not to go with her. It was heartbreaking for me to see a father giving away his daughter and later watching them dance together, knowing I would never have the opportunity to do either with Sally.

As our event grew closer, the demand for tickets surged. God and Sally were at work again. On the day of the event, Morgan and I hosted the member of Jo Dee's band at Quail Hollow. Afterwards, the evening could not have gone better. We owe so much to so many people for their help and dedication, including many of the employees of the Greater Charlotte YMCA community. They put their heart and soul into making it a special night. Jo Dee gave a memorable performance. Jimmie and Chani sat with us, as did Steve Cummings. Ron and his wife, Tamera, also came and sat nearby. Jo Dee closed with "Heaven Was Needing a Hero." I sat and listened with tears streaming down my face. I wasn't the only one crying.

Though we raised nearly $400,000 through our event, the effects of the financial crisis had major implications on our plans. We were still short of our goal, and no one wanted to move forward with construction until we were fully confident in our ability to finish the project and know it would be successful. Memberships at YMCAs were being dropped in large numbers due to the economy, and no one wanted to open Sally's Y and have it not be sustainable. Our vision would have to wait.

Jo and me with Jo Dee at the Sally's Y Gala

27

2009: A Year of Uncertainty and Reflection

⁓

In early 2009, Mac gave me a book written by Dr. David Cook, a noted sports psychologist, about a fictional professional golfer who had lost sight of what was important in life. Golf had become all-consuming and dictated every high and low in his life. Nothing else mattered. In *Golf's Sacred Journey: Seven Days at the Links of Utopia*, following a meltdown at a golf tournament, the main character ends up meeting a gentleman who takes him under his wing and over seven days, helps him come to understand the most important thing in life is to have faith and trust in God and His Son, Jesus Christ, and not his all-consuming worship of golf. Should he place them first, golf would take care of itself.

As many who have loved the game of golf and allowed it to impact their state of mind, I was profoundly moved by the book. While in many ways I had come to this conclusion after losing Sally and recognizing the changes in myself from my heartbreak, I knew it still spoke to me and reinforced that golf is just a game—nothing more—and I must never lose sight of this fact. I thanked Mac for giving it to me and told him how its message had resonated with me. Mac said it had affected him in the same way and he had given a copy to many golfer friends who also had the same experience. We decided to invite Dr. Cook to address a group at Quail Hollow. He came in April and gave a very moving talk to around 100 people. Given all that was taking place at the time, his message of hope was timely.

As the year progressed, the world economy teetered on the verge of total collapse. Businesses were failing and people who once felt financially secure were declaring bankruptcy. Some of the pledges made toward Sally's Y could not be fulfilled. Jo and I continued to hope that a facility of some size could be built once we weathered the financial crisis, and we trusted the Y's leadership to make the final decision.

Given this backdrop, I wavered about whether I should plan to play any of the courses until things improved. I also had developed an issue with my right knee that was a cause for concern. After much thought, I finally decided to go in September and play all the courses across the lower half of Ireland. Two weeks before I was to leave, I had arthroscopic surgery to repair torn cartilage in my knee. My doctor, Glenn Perry, told me I wouldn't be 100 percent, but I would be fine to make the trip.

If there was such a thing as a silver lining, and I use that term respectfully, it's that many clubs across the British Isles had dropped their greens fees in order to attract more outside play. Like virtually every other business, golf was feeling the effects of the downturn. I was surprised by the low rates I found on some club websites and hotels.

I started on September 1and went immediately from Shannon to Ballybunion with a goal of playing my way along the southeastern part of the country. I would work my way to Old Head, then play up toward Dublin, where I could play some courses I had not previously played. Almost immediately into my round at Ballybunion, my knee began to swell after walking up and down the dunes that Ballybunion is laid through. I could hardly bend it and thought my trip would begin and end here.

I called Glenn when I reached my hotel, and he assured me I would not do any additional damage to my knee. He suggested I repeatedly ice it through the night. By the next morning the swelling had subsided, but my knee was still tight. I decided to try to play Dooks Golf Club, and thankfully my knee loosened up as I played. I suddenly had hope for the remainder of my trip.

Staying in Waterville that evening, I iced my knee again, and by the next morning it felt much better. Waterville was a course I'd heard and read so much about, I was very excited to play it for the first time. I wasn't disappointed.

From there, I headed to Tralee, a course about which I'd heard mixed reviews. It wasn't Waterville, for sure, but I thoroughly enjoyed it. Its back nine has some of the best holes I've played anywhere, including the par-4 12th, which is spectacular and as tough as it looks.

Next on my itinerary was Old Head. I arrived around 7:30 a.m. as the sun was rising. It was magnificent and reminded me of Sally and her love of glorious sunrises and sunsets. I was first off and had the course to myself, an almost magical feeling. On several tees, I drove my balls out into the Atlantic. The course is spectacular, as it is perched atop cliffs. Photographs can't do it justice. I then worked my way up the east coast to Dublin, where I spent several nights before flying home.

In the last quarter of 2009, the Y's leadership decided to do a new feasibility study, focusing on what residents in East Lincoln would now support. The original study had shown strong membership numbers to support a 35,000-square-foot facility that included a full gymnasium and indoor pool with dues revenue to support it. The new economy forced a significant reevaluation. The feasibility study suggested a much smaller facility—14,000 square feet with a smaller gym and no indoor pool.

Jo and I hoped and prayed that we could move forward at some point, even if Sally's Y wouldn't be as big as we first imagined. We shared our desire with the Y leadership but stressed that we didn't want to do anything until we could be sure it would be successful and could become an integral part of the community. We didn't want Sally's name attached to a failed venture. That would be devastating to us. We believed we'd see our dream become a reality, even if it took more time and struggle than we first envisioned.

As 2009 came to a close, it had now been over five years since the accident. Yet, not a day passed without my thinking of Sally and where she might be in life. I continued to return to Machpelah each week to place roses and sunflowers, and I cried just as hard when I left as the first time I brought them in 2004. While there is truth in the saying "Time heals all wounds," the pain from the wound of losing a child remains ever present. In my humble opinion, it is deeper and more permanent and never completely heals. When you lose a child, unlike any other loss, a part of you has been lost forever and can never be replaced. I remember reading something Rose Kennedy, the mother of President Kennedy, said that continued to resonate with me. Besides President Kennedy, she buried three other children in her lifetime, all involving tragic circumstances. In her memoir, when discussing the loss of her children she said, "It has been said, 'time heals all wounds.' I do not agree. The wounds remain. In time, the mind, protecting its sanity, covers them with scar tissue and the pain lessens. But it is never gone."

As I considered where I stood with my own loss, I determined I would continue on my walk and hope that in time, as Mrs. Kennedy offered, enough scar tissue would cover my wound and lessen the pain enough for me to obtain final peace of the void left by Sally.

28

2010:
A Formative Year

~⌒~

As 2010 opened, the Greater Charlotte YMCA leadership voted and approved to begin construction of Sally's Y. We got the good news from Mary Tucker, who had been at our side from the start. It was incredibly happy news for Jo and me to know that our hopes and prayers of preserving and perpetuating Sally's beautiful legacy to help others had been answered. Sally's Y would honor those values.

Construction began in April, and I'll never forget the emotion of walking the site with Jo as they began moving dirt. All the dreaming and planning was finally being turned into something real. Since the night I awoke with the idea of building a Y to honor Sally and my chance meeting with Andy Calhoun the next morning, God and Sally had led us to this moment.

It was indeed a powerful and meaningful moment, and as Mrs. Kennedy had suggested, it provided more scar tissue over the wound. However, a new development in our family brought the specter of losing a child back into our lives. In early summer, Reynolds informed us he planned to enlist in the marines and would

report to Officer's Candidate School that fall. While incredibly proud of him, the thought of losing another child, even under such honorable circumstances, was gut wrenching. I wasn't sure I could handle it if we lost another child. I still don't know. I can only trust that God does not put more on us than we can bear. As the summer wound down, I decided to return to Scotland and continue my walk in early October. The day before I left, Reynolds left for Quantico. It was a very emotional moment for everyone.

En route to Glasgow the next day, as I was making a connection at Gatwick, I suddenly remembered that Jo had asked to try my putter while we were playing at Cowan's Ford. I didn't remember her putting it back in my bag. That's because she hadn't.

My first round was at Machrihanish Dunes on the Kintyre Peninsula, a truly spectacular part of Scotland. Checking in, I explained my putter dilemma to an assistant pro and asked if he might have one I could use for 18 holes. He ducked into the back, then emerged with a Scotty Cameron of his own, similar to the Cameron Newport model I'd left back in North Carolina. When I was done, I remembered to return the borrowed putter and thanked the assistant pro.

The architect and developer at Machrihanish Dunes had gone to great lengths to leave as much land as possible undisturbed. God had indeed laid out a golf course here, and he'd done a marvelous job of finding His work and placing the course among some magnificent dunes. It was an old-fashioned design, one that laid the course on and around what was there rather than creating land forms. It's probably the finest example of a true links course built in recent years. Machrihanish Golf Club was next on my list, and it was a favorite from having played it before. It coincided with the final day of the Ryder Cup matches at Celtic Manor in Wales. The Europeans were winning again by a big margin when the final day began. As I was putting on my shoes before playing, several men came out of the clubhouse shaking their heads. I asked how the Ryder Cup was coming and they told me the Americans were in the midst of a comeback. The outcome still hung in doubt. I was tempted to watch the end but instead decided to head out and play. I again had to explain my putter dilemma to a female assistant pro, and asked if she might have a putter I could borrow. Again, she offered a Scotty Cameron just like mine. *How lucky can you be?* I thought.

As I made my way around Machrihanish Golf Club, the wind steadily increased to the point that even the seagulls had a hard time standing in the gusts. I was reminded of a comment Nick Faldo made prior to an Open Championship in the 1990s when he said, "It blew so hard even the gulls walked." That's the kind of day I'd caught.

When I finished, I returned the putter and asked the outcome of the Ryder Cup. The assistant pro told me the Europeans barely held on and that Hunter Mahan had chunked a late chip shot at a critical moment in what would be the Cup's decisive match, a 3 & 1 loss to Graeme McDowell.

A five-hour drive the next morning preceded a round at Tain, where I borrowed another putter. This time, it was an off brand. After finishing my round, I again stayed at the Morangie House. The next morning I drove to the northernmost course in Scotland at Durness. The drive itself was worth the effort, rolling through some of the most dramatic scenery you'll find anywhere in the world. While it is only a nine-hole course, the setting is magical and the course itself is not a bad test. I was again able to borrow a putter from a lady who had just finished playing. She asked that I put it behind the door in the ladies locker room when I finished.

The putter

Durness Golf Club

My luck with putters soon ran out. At Reay, my next stop, the clubhouse was closed and the parking lot was empty. There was an honesty box, but there was no one to lend me a putter. I would have to improvise. I started putting with a 4-iron, but that didn't work very well. On the third hole, I used my 19-degree hybrid, gripping down on it and holding it off the ground so I could use its leading edge. I could make solid contact, but distance control was a challenge. The more I putted with my hybrid, though, the more comfortable I became with it. I decided to stick with it for the remainder of my trip, and I got to the point where I was putting better with the hybrid than I did with the putter I'd left at home.

When I played with a member who had asked me to join him at Nairn Dunbar, he offered to let me use his putter. After seeing me hole a handful of putts with my hybrid, however, he suggested I let my wife keep my putter and stick with the hybrid. What's that old saying? Necessity is the mother of invention?

During this trip, I had another funny moment like Mac and I had had during our excursion. When I showed up at Strathlene Buckie Golf Club, the parking lot was full and I noticed a group of ladies preparing to tee off. It was becoming a recurring theme in my travels—I continually showed up during ladies' competitions. I love ladies and I love golf, but I don't love playing a one-some behind their competitions.

A sign at the front door directed golfers to pay their greens fees at the bar on the second floor. Walking up the stairs, I could hear a large group of men talking. The place went stone quiet when I walked in, and all eyes were on me as I approached the bartender. With everyone watching me and wondering why I was there, I said in a nervous voice, "I happened to be in the area and thought I'd come in and see if I could play." The bartender, leaning on his bar, looked at me in disbelief.

Finally, after realizing I was serious, he said, "Oh sure, sure! The greens fees are 15 pounds." I paid immediately and asked when I could tee off. "Right now," the bartender told me. Then he turned around, opened a window, and yelled at the ladies preparing to tee off, "Hey, we've got an American who wants to play and you need to let him go off in front of you."

The clubhouse at Strathlene Buckie

By the time I arrived at the first tee with my clubs, the ladies were looking at me and they didn't appear to be happy. No one spoke. I teed up my ball, praying that I would hit a good tee shot and I could get the heck out of there. Fortunately, I ripped one of the best drives of my entire trip, prompting one of the ladies to say, "You may play in front of us." I was halfway down the second hole before their first group reached their tee shots on No. 1.

Over the course of this trip, I drove more than 2,000 miles. I'd begun by driving to the end of the Kintyre Peninsula, then played my way from the most northern course on the Scottish mainland all the way around to Edinburgh. I'd seen so much of the country I could almost be a Scottish tour guide. It was the most driving I'd done on a single trip, but I would do more in the future. There was a pleasure in the driving because the scenery was beautiful, even magnificent in places. I had collected many wonderful memories while playing 24 courses, most of them new to me.

When I returned home, Jo said she'd like to accompany me on my future trips if I was okay with that. I had always wanted her to join me in time, and I now felt like the timing was right. While still uncertain whether I'd play the remaining courses on my list, having her there would ensure she was with me when I finished. The initiation of construction on Sally's Y had brought a measure of closure for both of us. Jo had also ensured that Grace's memory would not be forgotten either. Members of Jo's family had donated money to have the chapel at Sally's Y named for Grace. It would be called Grace's Chapel. Whether both represented final closure, I would wait and see after Sally's Y opened and I decided whether to continue playing.

In December, Reynolds was commissioned a 2nd Lieutenant in the US Marines, and it was a proud and happy day for our family. He couldn't share many details with us, but from what he did share, it seemed his OCS training followed by Infantry Officer's School training was nearly as demanding as Navy Seal training. Only a small number of the soldiers who begin make it through to the end. Reynolds was one of those, and it was a proud moment, knowing our little boy had become a man.

29

New Life

At 8:08 a.m. on January 8, 2011, the ribbon was cut and Sally's Y opened.

Jo and me with Andy Calhoun as the
doors open for Sally's Y

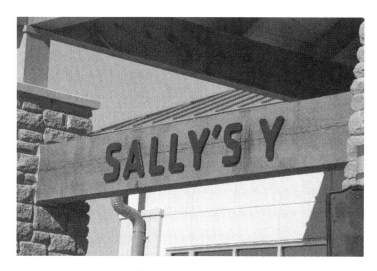

It was a moment of almost indescribable joy, pride, and sad-ness, all rolled into one enormous emotional package. We had set out to do something big and impactful, and we had done it despite the challenges. The number of people to whom we owe so much is enormous. There were contributions big and small, expected and unexpected, and they all made a difference. Without the seemingly tireless work of Mary, Dean, and Ron, and the financial support of the Cummings, the Keiths, my brothers Allison and Walter, and our sister Caroline, Sally's Y could not have happened. A memory of one. A vision for all. That had been our slogan, and finally it was our reality.

As I stood with Jo in the lobby after the ribbon cutting with tears in our eyes watching all the children running around, the significance of this moment was powerful and satisfying. Sally's spirit was indeed living on in the joy we were witnessing in these children. I knew God, Sally, and Grace were all smiling. Yet, as I processed whether this represented the final point in my walk and the last layer of scar tissue God intended for me, I sensed I had not yet obtained the full closure I so desperately sought. I continued to feel in time there would be a point when I knew I had found it. There would be no doubt what that peace would be, and I would find it on my walk. I also found comfort that Jo would be there with me the rest of the way.

With the decision to continue on, I began putting together the final version of my list of courses. Ever since I first compiled my list, it had undergone many revisions, some on the fly. Now, though, I needed to come as close to a final list as possible. Since I had expanded the original list beyond those in Mr. Steel's book to include many others, several new courses had opened or were under construction that fell in my categories, including Donald Trump's course in north Aberdeen. It was scheduled to open within a year. I decided Trump's new course would be the last course on my list and the last one I would play, providing a bit of symmetry to my travels.

To help finalize my list I used a book that had been published in 2010 called *True Links*. It was a collaborative effort by George Peper, former editor of *Golf Magazine,* and Malcolm Campbell, former editor of *Golf Monthly*, a European golf magazine. They outlined in their book what they deemed the real definition and description of a true links course and then created their own list of such courses throughout the world. It's a beautiful book with incredible photographs of courses on their list and in my opinion is, with Mr. Steel's book, the nearest thing to an authoritative source that includes a list of these types of courses.

Over the next couple of months I reviewed their list of courses located in the British Isles and compared it to mine. Knowing my list was longer because I'd included clifftop or seaside courses, I was still intrigued by the comparison. I found a small number of courses that I definitely considered a true links course, which they did not include, and some they classified as true links that I definitely considered more in the category of a clifftop or simply a seaside course. I think it would be fair to conclude that while certain courses are indisputable in their category, some are more difficult to place, adding an element of subjectivity to the process. I would later have the opportunity to discuss this observation with Mr. Peper, and he concurred with my conclusion.

Based on this effort, my list now stood at 292. My challenge would be planning how best to play the various courses in each country I still had not played. Until this point, I had picked and played courses in the same general area while not having a true master plan, as I never contemplated the possibility I might finish playing all the courses. Now with the list dwindling down, I knew I needed a plan to find the most practical way to finish—if that should be how it worked out.

As it stood I had the fewest courses to play in Ireland, so that's where Jo and I would begin. My thought was that hopefully by the end of this trip I could check Ireland off the list entirely. Based on my review using the book, I had learned that several of the more prominent or championship courses where I'd played also had a second 18, or at least another 9 holes. I hadn't played several of those and it created a quandary. If I considered them links, clifftop, or seaside layouts, I had to play them. Getting to all the courses on my list proved easier said than done.

In late September, Jo and I flew to Shannon and would first head to the Moy House in Lahinch, a place I'd fallen in love with on my stay in 2007. During my review and attempt to finalize my list, I learned that Lahinch had a second course called Castle across the road from the Old Course. Given my decision to play all the courses that fell into one of my categories, I needed to play it. How I'd missed it before I don't know. Even though I had already played it, we headed to Northern Ireland to play Royal Portrush

Dunluce—a favorite for both of us. I couldn't help but remember that moment in 2004 on the first tee when I marked my ball with Sally's initials and birthdate. The thought of it again brought out a lot of emotion.

The next morning after again staying at Ard Tara, we drove to east of Belfast to play Kirkistown Castle. While we were having lunch following our round, the club secretary approached us and asked what had brought us to his club and where we played at home. When we mentioned we were members at Quail Hollow that got his attention, because it's where Rory McIlroy won his first PGA Tour event in 2010. The secretary was so taken with us and our connection to McIlroy that he had us pose for a photograph for the club newsletter.

That afternoon, we headed to Newcastle to play County Down the next day. First, however, we would play Ardglass. The weather turned ugly very early in our round and we almost quit. At one point, we took cover under a rock outcropping along one hole to get out of the elements. Fortunately, the weather eased enough for

The wind meter in the clubhouse at Royal West Norfolk

us to finish. The next day, I played Royal County Down Annesley in the morning, then Jo joined me for a round at the championship course, one of the world's greatest courses. When we were done, all I had left to play in Ireland were a few courses near Dublin. I intended to play those the following year. That turned out to be wishful thinking.

We moved on to Edinburgh and played our way into the northeastern corner of England, finishing up at Royal West Norfolk, where the wind blew as hard as I've ever experienced on any golf course. Over the course of our trip, we played 18 courses.

When we returned, Reynolds and Jennifer invited us to dinner in Hickory, where they now lived. With the president's decision to first withdraw from Iraq and later from Afghanistan, Reynolds had been placed on reserve duty.

Before dinner they gave me a t-shirt that read, "I love my Pop." As I read it, I suddenly understood its significance. This was their special way of sharing that Jennifer was pregnant with their first child, our first grandchild! Her due date was early July 2012. They had already told Jo, but we were all emotional. It was a very special moment. They also shared that they would wait until the baby's birth to find out whether it was a girl or a boy. Still, I couldn't help thinking of Lisa Saunders' prayer. All I wanted, though, for Reynolds and Jennifer was a healthy baby. If it turned out to be a girl, that would be a bonus.

In early 2012, I was reminded again of how God works in wonderful ways. Leading up to Easter, Sally's beloved church, Grace Covenant, began holding services every Sunday at Sally's Y. With much trepidation, I decided to attend the first service with Jo. Sitting there with Jo and understanding the significance of the moment, the tears came again. This was all because of Sally. Her church, while not trying, had found another way to honor her memory, reaffirming our decision to build Sally's Y. Lives were being changed by the Y, and now her church was changing lives under the same roof. God is in control. I would never doubt it.

In mid-May, Jo and I headed back to Scotland for our most memorable trip to the British Isles, if not the most memorable trip of our marriage. It was one memory after another, a trip that will stay with us forever. We flew into Inverness and stayed one night at the Golf View Hotel in Nairn before moving on to the Morangie House Hotel in Tain. Over the next several days, we played Hopeman, Castle Stewart, Tarbat, and the Struie course at Royal Dornoch.

We then drove north to Thurso and took a ferry to the Orkney Islands. We had heard much about the islands and decided to make the effort to go there, not just for golf but also to visit. It was an incredible place, filled with gorgeous scenery and rich in ancient history.

After returning to Thurso, we returned to the Morangie House for one night before driving to play Gairloch Golf Club. We then turned south to the Isle of Skye to play Isle of Skye Golf Club and Traigh Golf Club. After spending the night in Ulg at the western end of the Isle of Skye, we took the early morning ferry to Isle of Lewis to begin our drive south through the Outer Hebrides Islands of Scotland. I can't do justice in words to describe the magnificence of these islands. The scenery is mesmerizing. Just when you think you've seen the best the islands can offer, you see something else even better.

We were there to play golf, and our first stop was the Isle of Harris Golf Club, a nine-hole course with a dramatic setting. It didn't matter that the weather was lousy when we arrived, we headed out anyway. We had grown accustomed to foul weather; it's part of the so-called charm of links golf. As we were putting on our rain suits, I noticed several children peering down at us from the house beside the parking lot, and I mentioned it to Jo. We could only imagine what they thought of us as we got ready to go out in such nasty weather. We laughed then and even now when we remember that moment.

Undeterred, we continued south, taking ferry rides before eventually arriving in North Uist and driving to South Uist to play Askernish Golf Club. I had read stories about a course located there, originally designed by Old Tom Morris. The course, according to the stories, had been abandoned, but in recent years it had been resurrected. It was described as a true links, and it had Old Tom Morris's fingerprints on it. I was hooked by the possibilities.

When we arrived, I had a sense about the place that reminded me of how I felt when I drove into St. Andrews for the first time, seeing the R&A clubhouse awash in sunshine. It was a snapshot moment that had stayed with me. Here, I felt it again. This could be something special.

While we were unloading our clubs, a West Highland terrier greeted us. We learned in the pro shop that his name was Snowflake, and Snowflake liked us so much he walked most of the first nine holes with us.

As we made our away around Askernish, the two of us had a growing sense that this course was indeed something special. It was the purest example of a true championship links I'd ever played, even more than the Old Course at St. Andrews, in my opinion. It was as if the course was built exactly as God intended it to be designed, laid perfectly across the land that existed. As I said earlier, pure links are discovered, not manufactured. The Old Course was originally that way, but through the years and with the advent of modern maintenance methods, man's influence has subtly softened and changed the character of the course, taking away a bit of its wild, untamed nature. The effort to get to Askernish was worth the trouble, and we hope someday to go back. I just hope those in charge of its care keep it the way it is and don't allow its quality to be diminished as it attracts more attention and players.

After a night at the Polochar Inn, we took the ferry to the Isle of Barra. As we were departing the ferry, I saw a signpost to the airport. I told Jo that I'd read the airport's runway was located on the beach and accessible only during low tide. Not exactly O'Hare International Airport. The novelty was too much to pass up, so we drove to the airport hoping to see a plane land on the beach. We weren't disappointed.

After watching the FLYBE flight land and take off, we drove to the Isle of Barra Golf Club, a nine-hole course that is still in its wildest form. How wild? We had to play through several herds of cattle during the round. You don't get that everywhere. On the tee closest to the ocean, I again pulled out one of my logo balls and hit it away, leaving a little bit of Sally there.

After we finished playing, we spent the night in Castlebay. The next morning we took a six-hour ferry ride to Oban, where we would spend the night. The next morning we planned to head to the Isle of Colonsay. Given our schedule, we needed a short flight on a small carrier called Hebridean Air, which no one would confuse with American Airlines. It is essentially the only way on or off the isle, unless you have your own boat or catch the occasional ferry.

It was so remote that there was not a car rental service available, so I emailed the website that promoted the island seeking advice. I received a message telling me the golf course was adjacent to the small airport, and the man who responded said he'd be happy to show us around the island after we finished playing and were waiting for our return flight.

After landing, Jo and I grabbed our clubs and headed outside in the direction we'd been pointed by an airport attendant. We looked around and saw no sign of a golf course. We were in a remote corner of the world looking for a golf course we'd been told was there but couldn't find. Finally, we saw a flag in the distance and walked toward it. The grass around the flag looked no different than fairway grass, but at least we'd found evidence of the golf course. Exactly where you played from and where you went remained a mystery to us. Fortunately, we saw the humor in our situation as we began walking toward a nearby road. We hoped it would lead us to a parking lot, if nothing else.

As we reached the parking lot, the man who had responded to my email pulled in and welcomed us to Colonsay. He showed us a monument on the grounds that detailed the course layout, then told us he'd be back in 90 minutes to meet us. Off we went. It was an experience for sure. There is wild and then there's really wild, in terms of course design. Colonsay was really wild. As for my belief that true links are discovered rather than manufactured, it's safe to say Colonsay is still being discovered.

We finished our short round, toured the island, and were on our way again, flying back to Oban, having had a truly unique experience. We next played Dunaverty Golf Club and Carradale Golf Club before heading south into England to play Burnham and Berrow. It was time to go home again, but on the drive back to Gatwick, we passed by Stonehenge, a final memory on a trip full of many.

On July 2, 2012, Jennifer gave birth to a beautiful baby girl whom they named Victoria McKenzie. Jo and I now had a granddaughter. It's difficult for me to describe the emotions of becoming a grandparent, particularly having a granddaughter. Thinking back to the evening when we stood at Machpelah following the service for Sally and Grace, it had seemed the sun had been setting in our lives for such a long time. Now, finally, it seemed the sun was rising. God had answered Reverend Lisa Saunders' prayer that someday I might have a granddaughter.

That fall, Jo and I flew to Ireland to play the remaining courses there. That was the plan anyway.

We began in Northern Ireland, where we played the Riverside and Old Course at Portstewart followed by the Bann course at Castlerock. After making a return visit to Royal Portush, we were finished in Northern Ireland. We then stayed for several nights in the northern part of Ireland at the Rathmullen House. For years I'd read about a course called St. Patrick's that was under construction near Rosapenna. It had an active website, but when I sent messages

I never heard anything back. I suggested to Jo that we drive around to see if we could find the course. Eventually we found what was intended to be a course, but construction had been stopped some time ago. You could see some of the fairways and an occasional green complex. It's an incredible piece of property, and I hope someday it will be finished because it has great potential. Since it wasn't an option to play, we went on to play Portsalon and Narin and Portnoo.

That left me with just three courses left to play in Ireland, and we headed to Dublin to play them. First was Rush Golf Club, followed by Corballis Golf Links, both excellent nine-hole courses. All that remained was the nine-hole course at Portmarnock called the Yellow. I'd played the Championship course at Portmarnock but not this one. When I finished, I had Jo snap a photo of me holding the flag on the ninth green. I'd played my way around Ireland, and we had a proper celebration with a couple of pints in the bar given this personal milestone. However, fate would later intervene and I would have to come back to finish a second time.

30

Back to the British Isles

~

As 2013 began, Jo offered to keep our granddaughter as much as possible to help Reynolds and Jennifer. It's what grandparents do, and it's a great blessing. We were calling our granddaughter McKenzie (Sally's middle name) while Jennifer's family called her Victoria. In time, we would let Victoria McKenzie tell us what she wanted to be called. In the meantime, as I'd done with all our children, I found a nickname for her. After a few months with her in our life and seeing and feeling the joy she brought, I knew McKenzie was my Sunshine.

With her new grandmotherly responsibilities, the failing health of her father, and a planned trip to Israel with her bible study group, Jo decided I should make my proposed springtime trip without her. Based on the list I compiled in 2011 and the courses I had played since, I still had approximately 70 courses to play. Given my original thought in 2004 that I would allow myself up to 10 years to find the peace I hoped to find on my walk, I realized I needed to play as many as I could that spring and possibly return in the fall to play approximately the last 10 courses in 2014 with Jo.

In February, as I began to lay out a roadmap on how to do this, I happened to pick up another of my favorite golf books by Lawrence Casey Lambrecht, entitled *Emerald Gems*. As I looked through it, I discovered there was a nine-course at County Sligo called Bomore in addition to the Championship course. I'd played the Championship but not the Bomore. Upon discovering this, I immediately had that "deer in the headlights" look when I realized another course in Ireland belonged on my list but I hadn't played it. *Should I ignore it or should I return to Ireland again?* It was my list.

After much thought, I decided to make sure Bomore was the only course I hadn't played in Ireland before making a final decision on what to do. Digging deep into my various reference materials, I discovered another nine-hole course at Enniscrone and an additional nine holes at Rosslare I hadn't played. Apparently, I wasn't finished in Ireland.

I also had to consider that if I was finding late additions to my list of Irish courses, I needed to be certain there were no more surprises like this waiting for me. I needed finality to my list so that in the end there would be closure and sense of completion, which might bring its own measure of peace. I was also still bothered by my decision not to play St. David's City and only partially playing Plye and Kenfig in Wales in 2006.

Also, to add these courses meant going back to Ireland and posed challenges to my desire to finish in 2014. Still not sure what to do, I decided to at least see if there was a practical way to return to Ireland to truly finish and then make my way to England, where I had planned to start in the spring. As I checked ferry routes from Ireland, I was overwhelmed with emotion when I saw there was a ferry from Rosslare to Fishguard in the south of Wales. As I looked over the map to find Fishguard, I was again filled with emotion. I saw that St. David's City was less than an hour from the Fishguard port. God and Sally were showing me the way to truly finish. In that moment, I knew I was meant to finish the list I had created.

Still I had to find a way to the northwest area of Ireland to play the nine-hole courses at County Sligo and Enniscrone. After considering the flight schedules, I determined that the best thing to do would be to fly into Dublin, then drive four hours across Ireland to first play County Sligo that afternoon, and then drive to Enniscrone, spend the night nearby, and drive the following day six hours to Rosslare to play there that afternoon. I could spend the night and catch the early morning ferry to Wales. I now had my path to truly finish in both countries the courses on my list. I also found one additional course in Wales called Newport that was also less than an hour from the ferry port.

In March, Sally's Y held its first Easter prayer breakfast, and Jim Morgan, who was board chair of the entire Y organization in 2004, was the guest speaker. Jo was in Israel, so I attended without her. As I listened to Jim's inspirational and moving message, I again found myself overcome with emotion, remembering our first meeting with Andy and Jim when we suggested the idea to build Sally's Y. Like Grace Covenant's decision to open a church in Sally's Y, here was a man who had played such an important and meaningful role in our efforts, speaking during Holy Week nine years after our world had gone dark.

Jim finished his talk with the message, "Walk with Him. Listen to Him." I thought of my days on the golf courses across the ocean as I walked and all the times I'd talked to God and Sally. The message meant so much to me that I went to Quail Hollow that afternoon and arranged to have it stitched into the golf bag I took on my trips.

In May, a marathon golf trip began. It would encompass driving more than 3,000 miles, taking six ferries, and playing 39 courses. I traveled through five countries—England, Scotland, Ireland, Northern Ireland, and Wales—over the course of my meandering path. For the second time, I completed playing all the courses on my list in Ireland. This time I was sure I had played them all. When I finished at Rosslare, I asked a gentleman in the golf shop to snap a photo of me on the ninth green. Before we could do that, the man's Jack Russell terrier named Rocco snatched one of my favorite head covers and tried to tear it apart. We spent several minutes chasing the dog to recover my head cover. Eventually, I got both my head cover and my photograph.

From Ireland, I took a ferry to Wales, where I played St. David's City, then Newport, and finally Pyle and Kenfig to complete my list of courses there. I moved on to the west country of England, by far the most beautiful part of the country. It's full of beautiful scenery and great golf courses. The only downside is, like in Wales, the courses tend to be spread out and the travel time between them adds to the length of a trip. Regrettably, I think that will keep many Americans from taking the time to play some outstanding courses in gorgeous settings.

When I reached the east coast, I played Frinton Golf Club, one of the courses I had not previously played. In my correspondence setting up my tee time, I learned that the head professional, Peter Taggart's son David, had done an internship with the greens superintendent at Quail Hollow. I introduced myself after my round, and he was so appreciative of my visit he gave me a bag tag as a thank you.

My journey then wound to the Southport area of England and up to the northwest coast of Scotland. I played Southerness again, then hopped on a ferry from Portpatrick into Belfast, where I played a round at Portstewart Strand before flying home from Dublin. I was fortunate to play so many good courses along the way in some of the most scenic areas in the world, and I appreciated the opportunity. Among the courses that really earned my respect were Trevose, Perranporth, Thurlstone, Rye Jubilee, and Seascale. Were it not for the massive power station right next to Seascale, it would certainly be more familiar to visiting golfers. Playing the holes closest to the nuclear facility at Seascale, I noticed an SUV inside the fence surrounding the facility. As I continued around the course, I had no doubt the occupants of the car were watching the lone golfer who was getting close to the facility. After watching me for 15 minutes, they finally pulled away.

31

The Final List

～

With the conclusion of this trip, I could see the end in sight. I flew home with only 31 courses remaining to be played. Unfortunately, the remaining courses on my list were spread across northern England and both coasts of Scotland, a large area to cover. I decided I would make two trips, one in the fall and another in May 2014, to complete my long walk. Jo and I would finish as I had planned in 2011 by playing Donald Trump's new links near Aberdeen.

Not long after returning home, however, I began to experience nerve pain down my right leg. I'd had successful back surgery in 1999 to repair a bad disc and a neck surgery for another bad disk in 2002. I'd been pain free since those surgeries and counted my blessings, knowing surgery doesn't always alleviate the pain for everyone and sometimes makes it worse.

I went to see Dr. Bruce Darden, who had done my two previous surgeries, and an MRI revealed I had severe compression at the site of my lower back surgery. In spite of a nerve block, the pain intensified. I wanted to make my fall trip but when the day arrived to leave, I couldn't. Instead of getting closer to my goal, I would have another surgery to hopefully alleviate the pain. Since I was having trouble standing, swinging a golf club was out of the question. Dr. Darden expressed confidence he could relieve my pain and I would make a 100 percent recovery within a month. While hopeful he was right, the unknowns associated with surgery brought questions and doubt that I would be able to finish playing all the courses on my list.

I had surgery in late October, and while the procedure was a success, I developed a staph infection followed by blood clots from the pic line they'd inserted in my arm to administer the antibiotics. My four-week recovery became 12 weeks with an additional surgery. In late January 2014, Dr. Darden finally gave me clearance to play again. When I began hitting balls, I had trouble feeling loose and worried that I'd have to live with that feeling as a result of the surgeries. The thought of now being physically limited added to an internal struggle I had been confronting since 2004.

While I continued to play, the mental side of golf had changed for me after Sally's death. I slowly became aware in the months after the accident that I had lost my ability to handle pressure in every facet of my personal and business life. I hadn't always felt that way. I wasn't a risk-taker by nature, but I had thrived when the circumstances required me to perform, and most often I would rise to the moment. That confidence left me on April 4, 2004. I would play with friends, often because it was unavoidable, but I preferred playing alone or with only Jo. I could relax, and there was no pressure. Although there wasn't any real pressure playing a casual round with friends, undeniably, it had begun to feel that way.

This latest surgery and the potential of now being physically challenged left me in a deep, dark place with my golf. I needed help, so I went to see Bruce Sudderth at Gaston Country Club.

I'd worked with him for more than 20 years, but it had been more than a year since I last visited him. He's a brilliant teacher with an approach built on old-school fundamentals and simplifying the swing. Bruce has a gift for getting his message across in an encouraging manner, cutting through the clutter and cleansing your mind of the bothersome thoughts that gather when the game is fighting you. On top of his teaching ability, he is one of the finest people I know, and beyond helping me with golf, I hoped he could help me with the mental battle I was fighting in my head about playing with others.

I had forgotten how to release the club, and even before my surgery, I had begun to lose distance—and not just because I was getting older. Bruce took me back to the most basic level, reminding me what it feels like to let the club drop and release. We worked together over three months in preparation for my trip, and while I saw progress, I still didn't trust my swing. That wasn't going to stop me from finishing what I had started, though.

Since my trip the previous summer and the decision not to go back in the fall, I still had 31 courses remaining to play. Now, I wanted to finish them in one trip. Given Jo's continued responsibility in helping to care for McKenzie, we decided I would leave on May 8 and play on my own. Then, she would join me near the end to play the last three. After we played the final course on my list, we planned to spend a couple of nights at the Tulchan Lodge and then head north to play Royal Dornoch and a few other courses again.

As I was leaving home for the airport, Reynolds brought McKenzie out to say goodbye. Jo was taking me to the airport, and as we were backing out of our driveway, Reynolds stood with McKenzie waving goodbye. I waved back and McKenzie started to cry, holding her little arms out and calling, "Pop, Pop," her nickname for me.

Jo looked at me and said, "That must make you feel good." While trying to suppress the well of emotion building inside, I managed to say, "You just don't know." My heart was in my throat and tears were in my eyes. I was again staring through the windshield of our Suburban, just like I had on the night of April 4, 2004. I also remembered staring through the windshield when the mysterious bright light illuminated my car on the drive to Sea Island and looking out the windshield of Sally's car when I saw the bumper sticker that bothered me so much. It was all coming together. The peace God had intended was right in front of me. My granddaughter. Our granddaughter.

I was leaving to finish a deeply personal journey that had been born out of my grief over losing my sweet Sally, and God was now making sure I knew *where* I'd find that peace when I finished my long walk. It was the circle of life. I had much to look forward to when I returned.

The last leg of my walk began when I landed in Manchester and was greeted by a chilly, overcast day. I was headed to the east coast of England to play the courses remaining on my list before finishing in Scotland. Because my plane had been late arriving, I had to scratch a planned round the first afternoon, immediately forcing me to rework my schedule. I had to work back from the end, knowing Jo and I had an 8:45 a.m. tee time on Saturday, May 24, at Trump International, the final course on my list. Jo would fly into Aberdeen on May 22, and I needed to have played all but three courses on my list by then. I could do that.

Driving to Whitby for my first round, I saw storm clouds approaching from the west. I'd been making these golf trips since 1986 and miraculously had never encountered a storm or rain delay. I'd forged on despite the conditions. I'd also never seen lightning in the British Isles and only rarely heard the rumble of thunder, usually distant. There's a first time for everything, I suppose. When I reached Whitby, the lightning began popping all around. People were still playing, though. I couldn't believe it. Remembering my Northern Ireland bus trip, I wasn't about to repeat a case of real dumb. I had no intention of playing in lightning. I stayed in the clubhouse and watched the golfers gradually make their way in from the course. I waited four hours, sitting through more than one intense storm, and was eventually rewarded when the weather improved. The late start only added to my concern about getting all the rounds in I'd planned. I decided not to worry about that while playing Whitby. I would figure out the logistics that evening.

I was thrown another curveball on Sunday when, after playing Cleveland, my plan to play Hartlepool was scuttled because of a competition. I was still early in my trip but the challenges were mounting. I had to figure out how to play 16 courses over the upcoming week, because I was booked to catch a ferry to the Isle of Mull the following Sunday to play the two courses there. The weather wasn't helping. The storms ceased but it remained cloudy, cold, and windy with occasional rain.

I got in 45 holes on Monday at Hartlepool, Newbiggin, and then Warkworth, a nine-hole course. Tuesday was another 45-hole day, including Alnmouth, a nine-hole course, then Winterfield and Gullane No. 3. I was just getting warmed up. On Wednesday, I played the relatively new Renaissance Club with Jerry Sarvadi, who developed it. From there, I went down the road to play Craigelaw and drove around the Firth of Forth to play the Jubilee Course at St. Andrews before dark.

I was on a mission. I still had to play seven courses over the next three days and the weather forecast was calling for heavy rain on Saturday. There was the added complication of being a single at St. Andrews where you weren't allowed to book a tee time. I still needed to play the Eden, Strathyrum, and Castle courses as well. No one said it would be easy.

To that point, my golf had not been particularly good. I'd hit some decent shots, but I still hadn't gotten my distance back and I'd begun to believe I'd never regain it. It wasn't an encouraging thought. On Thursday, though, things began to improve while playing the Kittocks course at the Fairmont Hotel in St. Andrews. I hit a couple of good tee shots that had more crack to them than before. I had hope.

After lunch, I showed up at the Eden Course, asking the starter when I might be able to play. He pointed me to the tee and I was on my way. On the front nine, I sensed a different rhythm to my swing and I'd begun to release the club better. At the par-5 ninth, I crushed a drive, something I hadn't done in a long time. Then I ripped a great 3-wood into the green for a two-putt birdie. It was the first time in two years I'd reached a par-5 in two.

I played the back nine of the Eden course in 2-over, then went around the Strathyrum course in even par. It was like the training wheels Bruce had put on me in January were coming off. Golf was fun again. I texted Bruce immediately to let him know what was happening and to thank him. I still wasn't terribly confident and wasn't sure how I'd feel playing with any pressure on me but, as I told Bruce when I returned home, he'd helped me enjoy the game again.

I got up at six the next morning to hopefully beat everyone to the Castle Course. I was feeling the physical effects of having played 12 courses in four days but I had to finish by Saturday. I was first off at the Castle Course and, having heard mixed reviews about the newest course under the St. Andrews umbrella, I was looking forward to forming my own opinion. It didn't take me long to understand the mixed reviews.

From tee to green, there was plenty to like. The fairways were wide, the routing flowed nicely with the land, and the Castle Course offered some great views of St. Andrews from about three miles down the coast. The greens, however, were some of the worst-designed greens I'd ever played. I found myself standing in fairways feeling as if there was no place to hit my ball onto the green, which had far too much roll and some virtually impossible pin positions. If they would admit their mistake with the greens, tear them up, and rebuild them with significantly softer contours—like those at nearby Kingsbarns—they would match the rest of the course and give St. Andrews a course that people would look forward to playing.

From there, I drove down the narrow, winding road to Crail to play the Balcomie course, one of the oldest courses in the world. Honestly, I didn't care much about how I played. I was exhausted and all I wanted to do was finish and get back to my hotel. Fourteen courses in five days had wiped me out.

Finishing with a mid-morning tee time at the Fairmont Torrance course on Saturday was a piece of cake after what I'd put myself through. I was up at five on Sunday to make the five-hour drive to Oban to catch the ferry to the Isle of Mull. It poured rain the entire drive, poured on the ferry ride, and continued to pour while I played golf at the two nine-hole courses on the isle named Craignure and Tobermory. The courses were soaked, but I finished and hopped back on the ferry to Oban.

The rain had thankfully moved out by the following morning, when I again found myself on Hebridean Air flying to the Isle of Tiree to play the nine-hole course there. It reminded me of the Isle of Colonsay course, in that it was still in the process of being discovered and figuring out the routing was a challenge in itself.

After flying back to Oban and spending the night nearby, I headed south, where I caught two ferries to the Isle of Bute to play the nine-hole course there. I then took another ferry to Wemyss Bay and drove three hours to Carnoustie. I'd played the championship course at Carnoustie but not the Buddon or Burnside courses there. I played both of those on Wednesday plus the Ashludie course at Monifieth.

The good news was that after more than 1,500 miles of driving, five ferry rides, and almost more rounds than I could count, I was back on schedule. I could still finish as planned, though I needed to get in 27 holes the next morning before Jo would arrive in the afternoon in Aberdeen. Still, the pace I'd been keeping to finish and be in Aberdeen to meet Jo was gradually taking an overall toll. On several occasions while playing, I had to stop and remind myself where I was at that particular moment.

In Aberdeen, I played the municipal courses at Balnagask and the Kings. I'd been told the Kings Links was just nine holes, but I'd received bad information. It was a full 18-hole course. By the time I arrived at Balnagask, the bottom had fallen out. Rain fell as if it were coming out of a fire hose. Mine was the only car in the parking lot, and when I went to pay my greens fee, the man behind the window had a look of disbelief on his face. No one in their right mind would play in such nasty conditions. Of course, I wasn't in my right mind. I was on a quest.

I slogged my way around the course as the rain worsened and the temperature dropped. I was as miserable as I had ever been on a golf course. I finally finished around 11:30 a.m. Knowing Jo wasn't scheduled to land until 2:00 p.m., I felt I had enough time to get my round in at the Kings Links if I skipped lunch. That was assuming it was a nine-hole course and assuming I wouldn't get lost trying to find it.

I finally saw a sign for Kings Links and what appeared to be a golf hole behind a building that sure didn't look like a clubhouse. With the rain still falling, I pulled my clubs out of the car and headed around the building to what appeared to be the first tee. I saw no obvious place to pay a greens fee but I didn't care. If they wanted it, they could come find me.

Something didn't seem right about where I was and not just because my hands were so cold and wet that the club went farther than my ball on my first swing. After playing several "holes," I realized I was on the children's course and the real course was to my right. It wasn't nine holes. It was eighteen. Standing in the rain, I wasn't sure what to do. I had to get to the airport to pick up Jo.

When she arrived, we decided to eat in the airport. I told her my wet tale from the morning and said I would consider the few holes I played on the children's course as a substitute for playing the real thing. Without saying anything, Jo just looked at me. I knew from her look that I'd be going back, but I wasn't going back today, not with the way it continued to rain, and we were booked to play the nine-hole courses at Cruden Bay and Fraserburgh the following day. I'd done enough at Kings Links for today.

With an early start the next morning, we played the two nine-hole courses as planned. After lunch, we headed to Kings Links for me to truly play it. With the rain gone, we got it all in. All that was left was my final round at Trump International. We were on the tee at 8:45 the next morning, anxious to see the course that had drawn so much attention and local criticism. From the moment Trump announced his intention to build the course it had been ensnared in controversy. The fact that it was Trump building the course probably didn't help matters, but he was also building amid some of the most spectacular dunes in the world.

I had recently read a *Wall Street Journal* story that wasn't particularly positive, but I'd also read several other stories that gave the course high marks. I wanted to decide for myself. Plus, it was the last course on my list. It would be a special round for many reasons.

We weren't disappointed with the golf course. As we reached each tee, almost all of which were elevated, there was always a collective "Wow!" as we looked out at the next hole. The course had a massive scale to it, and it was staggeringly beautiful in spots. We kept waiting for a weak hole, but we never found one. Trump International deserves the highest praise.

In spots, there was some evidence of sand and soil being moved to create tee and green complexes. It fit my definition of a true links. God had routed this course through the massive dunes. Trump and Martin Hawtree had done a magnificent job discovering it.

As the round wound down, I kept thinking about how I felt, knowing this was the culmination of years of soul-searching. It was the 290th course on my list of 290. I was about to be finished.

Jo asked what I was feeling, and I couldn't feel much other than the joy of playing such a great golf course. When we reached the 18th tee, one of the assistant pros was standing there with another person. The tee was situated atop a massive dune, providing an incredible view of the finishing hole as well as much of the course. I'd carried my bag up the hill to prop my camera on it for a photograph. There were also several people walking along a nearby path, sightseeing at a course that had drawn so much attention. So much for having any privacy on the final hole of my long walk. Jo and I practically had a gallery.

Fortunately, both of us hit good tee shots. The assistant glanced at my clubs and, seeing the worn areas on some of the faces of my irons, remarked that I must know how to use them. Little did he know …

I would love to say I finished that last hole, a great par-5, by hitting four good shots and making a birdie. Instead, I pushed my second shot, then left my third short off the green. I pitched to within five feet but missed my par putt. Damn. So much for a storybook finish.

We casually walked off the green with little fanfare from the "gallery" still close by. We went inside for lunch and planned to toast the completion of this journey with a pint of Tennant's.

When we asked our server what kind of beer they had, she said just one—Trump's own brand. Of course. We should have known.

After finishing, we loaded up our clubs and began our drive to the Tulchan Lodge, where we would stay two nights. I was looking forward to a day off from golf, as we planned to play a few extra rounds in the Highlands before returning home, starting Monday at Royal Dornoch. As we drove away from Trump International, what I had expected to be a very profound emotional moment was absent. I wasn't sure what to make of it. The impact would come later.

32

Final Impact

~~

Driving to lunch the next day, I began to feel something building inside as I thought of Sally and my decision to play these courses and how I'd finally reached the end of my walk. I also thought about McKenzie and that moment as we pulled away from our home. Jo asked several times how I felt, and I just couldn't articulate my emotions.

The next morning, we headed to Dornoch to play our first post-round on our favorite course, and the weather settled in around us. I continued to think about what I'd done and the fact that I *was* done. I'd just spent nearly three weeks crisscrossing England and Scotland, rarely seeing the sun, in a mad dash to finish on this trip. I'd spent the last 10 years since the accident trying to find what peace God would grant me, acceptance of the loss of Sally, and a way to move forward. It had been a long and emotional walk since that first tee at Royal Portrush when I marked my ball with Sally's initials and birthdate. As we drove, all that transpired over these 10 years continued to settle in. My emotions were finally beginning to surface, and I realized I had nothing left to give. I didn't want to play another hole, much less another 18, even at Royal Dornoch. I was physically and emotionally exhausted. The profound emotional moment I had expected at Trump International was now coming out.

We had a 2:00 p.m. tee time, and after parking, we headed to the bar for lunch. Looking out the window at the first hole, it began pouring rain. As I had at the memorial service and the following Easter services, I locked my eyes on an object, this time a bunker in the first fairway, to try to hold it together. I knew if I looked at Jo, I would totally lose it. I knew also that no matter how much I tried, I was not going to find the emotional or physical strength to play. At least not today. The tank was empty. Yet, I didn't want to disappoint her. She had really been looking forward to playing here.

Jo could sense what was happening, and as I stared out the window, she said, "That's okay. You don't have to play. I understand. I'm still going to play and you can carry my bag and help me." All I could say as I continued to look out the window at that bunker was, "I'm sorry and thank you for understanding."

After lunch, we went to the car and got Jo's clubs and donned our waterproofs. Even though the rain continued, I didn't care. I couldn't imagine being anywhere else but there with Jo, walking our favorite golf course, carrying her bag. Unlike the day at Lahinch, when I was totally consumed with my own game and not losing my ball and not helping her in any way, this time I was able to give her my full and undivided help and attention. She deserved this moment. I owed it to her. She had spared me that night from something I doubt I could have recovered from and she had allowed me to come over here all these many times to grieve on my own. She had done that for me.

This was her time, and I wanted her to enjoy it. We had a

beautiful granddaughter at home who we both loved, and while nothing could or would fill the void in our lives and bring back our sweet Sally, I knew beyond any doubt McKenzie was the final peace God had granted us. As I'd always hoped, it had indeed come on my walk, when I saw her there with Reynolds crying and calling out her name for me. I realized we had so much to be thankful for. As we made our way around the course through the rain in Scotland, the sun was again shining on us.

Epilogue

~

Before leaving on my trip to play the final courses on my list, I decided to buy a smaller car to replace the Suburban I'd been driving for years. I'd focused on several makes and models but decided to wait until I came home to make my decision.

After our return, Jo and I went car shopping and to have dinner out one Saturday. We planned to look at a small Audi SUV, and on our way there, we came upon Hendrick BMW, where I'd bought several cars, including Sally's beloved 330i coupe, and had placed the order with her in early 2004 for a BMW SUV. I hadn't owned a BMW since 2006, because it reminded me too much of how she loved BMWs and of her car in particular. Jo suggested we stop in and take a look but emphasized we didn't have to buy one.

Entering the showroom, I noticed a model I hadn't seen before. I asked a salesman about it, and he told me BMW had taken the coupe model out of the 3 series and created a new 4 series. I was looking at a new model of Sally's car, a 428i.

Staring at the car, all I could think about was Sally. I could tell Jo was having the same thoughts. We continued looking, checking out the 5 series, but neither of us could quit looking at the 428i. Had God directed us here? Was it time to own one of these cars again?

We told the salesman we would think about it and get back to him in the future. If you've ever been in a car showroom and the salesman has figured out you're serious about buying a car, you know you're not getting away, at least not easily. They find all kinds of ways to keep you around, to delay your departure, hoping that they'll convince you to a buy a car right then.

We got as far as our car in the parking lot before feeling the tug to buy the 428i. It felt right for so many reasons. But we didn't buy it there. Using the Costco Auto Buying Program, we were able to find it at a significantly lower price at a dealer in Greenville, South Carolina. We chose a salmon/silver color, because we didn't want black and we didn't want it close to the color of Sally's car.

I can't help but think of Sally and how much I miss her each time I drive this BMW. As with so many other things, I knew after we purchased it that there was only one license plate for this car. It reads MISSUSUG.

Sally McKenzie Clark
– Through The Years

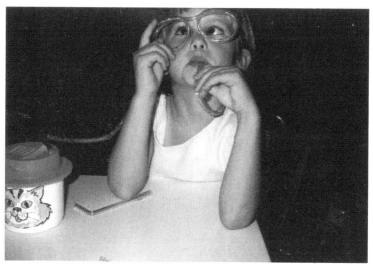

My Walk

Our Sunshine –
Victoria McKenzie Clark

LIST OF COURSES

England

Cornwall and Isles of Scilly	Type of Course	Last Year Played
Bude-Bude and North Cornwall Golf Club	Links	2013
Constantine Bay-Trevose	Links	2013
Lelant-West Cornwall Golf Club	True Links	2013
Mullion-Mullion Golf club	Clifftop	2013
Newquay-Newquay Golf Club	Links	2013
Perranporth-Perranporth Golf Club	True Links	2013
Portwrinkle-Whitsand Bay Hotel Golf and Country Club	Clifftop	2013
Rock- St. Enodoc	Links	2006
St. Mary's-Isles of Scilly Golf Club (9 Holes)	Clifftop	2013
Devon		
Axemouth-Axe Cliff Golf Club	Clifftop	2013
Budleigh Salterton-East Devon Golf Club	Clifftop	2013

Dawlish Warren-Warren Golf Club	Links	2013
Saunton-Saunton Golf Club East	True Links	2006
Saunton-Saunton Golf Club West	True Links	2006
Thurlestone-Thurlestone Golf Club	Links/Cliff-top	2013
Westward Ho!-Royal North Devon	True Links	2006
Somerset		
Burnham-on-Sea-Burham and Berrow Golf Club	True Links	2013
Minehead-Minehead and West Somerset Golf Club	Links/Seaside	2013
Weston-Super-Mare-Weston-Super-Mare Golf Club	Links/Seaside	2013
Dorset		
Bridgeport-Bridgeport and West Dorset	Clifftop	2013
Hampshire		
Barton-on-Sea Barton-on-Sea Golf Club	Clifftop	2013
Hayling Island-Hayling Golf Club	True Links	2005
Gosport-Gosport and Stokes Golf Club (9 Holes)	Links	2013

West Sussex		
Littlestone-Littlestone Golf Club	Links	2013

East Sussex		
Rye-Rye Golf Club-Old	True Links	2005
Rye-Rye Golf Club-Jubilee (11 Holes)	True Links	2013

Kent		
Deal-Royal Cinque Ports	True Links	2005
Hythe-Hythe Imperial Golf Club (9 Holes)	Seaside	2013
Broadstairs-North Foreland Golf Club	Seaside	2013
Littlestone-Littlestone Golf Club	Links	2005
Littlestone-Littlestone Warren Golf Club	Links	2013
Sandwich-Princes Golf Club (27 Holes)	True Links	2013
Sandwich-Royal St. Georges	True Links	2005
Kingsdown-Walmer and Kingsdown Golf Club	Clifftop	2013

Channel Islands		
Guesney-L'Ancresse Vale-Royal Guesney Golf Club	Links	2005
Jersey-Grouville-Royal Jersey Golf Club	Links	2005

Jersey-La Moye-La Moye Golf Club	Clifftop	2005
Isle of Wright		
Freshwater Bay Golf Club	Links/ Clifftop	2013
Essex		
Frinton-on-Sea-Frinton Golf Club	Seaside	2013
Suffolk		
Felixstowe-Felixstowe Ferry Golf Club	True Links	2005
Norfolk		
Brancaster-Royal West Norfolk	True Links	2011
Cromer-Royal Cromer	Links	2011
Gorleston on Sea-Gorleston Golf Club	Clifftop	2013
Great Yarmouth-Great Yarmouth and Caister	Links	2005
Hunstanton-Hunstanton Golf Club	True Links	2005
Sheringham-Sheringham Golf Club	Links/ Clifftop	2011
Lincolnshire		
Skegress-Seacroft	Links	2005

Sutton on Sea-Sandilands	True Links	2013
North Yorkshire		
Redcar-Cleveland Golf Club	Links	2014
Durham		
Seaton Carew-Seaton Carew Golf Club	True Links	2011
Hartlepool-Hartlepool Golf Club	Links	2014
Northumberland		
Alnmouth-Alnmouth Village (9 Holes)	Links/ Seaside	2014
Bamburgh-Bamburgh Castle Golf Club	Clifftop	2011
Berwick-upon-Tweed- Goswick	True Links	2011
Embleton-Dunstanburgh Castle Golf Club	Links	2011
Newbiggin-Newbiggin-By-The-Sea Golf Club	Links	2014
Seahouses-Seahouses Golf Club	Links/ Parkland	2011
Warkworth-Warkworth Golf Club (9 Holes)	Links	2014
Merseyside		
Blundellsands-West Lancashire Golf Club	Links	2008

Caldy-Caldy Golf Club	Links/ Seaside	2008
Formby-Formby Golf Club	Links	2008
Formby-Formby Ladies Golf Club	Links	2008
Hoylake-Royal Liverpool Golf Club	True Links	2008
Southport-The Hesketh Golf Club	Links/ Seaside	2008
Southport-Hillside Golf Club	Links	2008
Southport-Southport and Ainsdale	True Links	2008
Southport-Royal Birkdale Golf Club	True Links	2008
Southport-Southport Municipal Links	Links	2013
Wallasey-Wallasey Golf Club	True Links	2005
Wallasey-Leasowe Golf Club	Links	2008
Lancashire		
Fleetwood-Fleetwood Golf Club	Seaside	2008
Lytham St. Annes-Royal Lytham and St. Annes	Links/ Seaside	2008
Lytham St. Annes-St. Annes Old Links	True Links	2008
Lytham St. Annes-Fairhaven Golf Club	Links/ Parkland	2008
Cumbria		

Barrow-In-Furness-Furness Golf Club	Links	2008
Maryport-Maryport Golf Club	Links/Parkland	2013
Askam-In-Furness-Dunnerholme Golf Club (10 Holes)	Links	2008
St. Bees-St. Bees Golf Club (9 Holes)	Clifftop	2013
Seascale-Seascale Golf Club	True Links	2013
Silloth-Solloth-on-Solway Golf Club	True Links	2008

Isle of Man		
Castletown-Castletown Golf Links	True Links	2008
Port Erin-Rowany Golf Club	Links/Seaside	2008

Ireland

Donegal	Type of Course	Last Year Played
Ballyliffin-Ballyliffin-Old Links	True Links	2007
Ballyliffin-Ballyliffin-Glasedy Links	True Links	2014
Buncrana-North West Golf Club	Links	2007
Bundoran-Bundoran Golf Club	Links/Parkland	2007

Cruit Island-Cruit Island Golf Club (9 Holes)	Clifftop	2007
Dunfanaghy-Dunfanaghy Golf Club	Links	2007
Greencastle-Greencastle Golf Club	Links/Park-land	2007
Gweedore-Gweedore Golf Club (9 Holes)	Links	2007
Laghey-Donegal Golf Club	True Links	2007
Narin-Narin and Portnoo	True Links	2007
Portsalon-Portsalon Golf Club	True Links	2007
Rathmullan-Otway Golf Club (9 Holes)	Links/Park-land	2007
Rosapenna-Rosapenna Golf Club-Old Tom Morris	True Links	2007
Rosapenna-Rosapenna Golf Club-Sandy Hills Links	True Links	2007
*Carrigart-St. Patrick Golf Club-Maherama-gorgan (If ever completed.)	True Links	2012
*Carrigart-St. Patrick Golf Club-Tra-Mor (If ever completed.)	True Links	2012

County Silgo

Enniscrone-Enniscrone Golf Club	True Links	2014
Enniscrone-Enniscrone Golf Club-Scurmore	Links	2013
Silgo-County Silgo Golf Club	Links	2007
Sligo-County SligoGolf Club-Bomore	Links	2013

Sligo-Standhill Golf Club	Links	2007
County Clare		
Kilkee-Kilkee Golf Club	Clifftop	2007
Lahinch-Lahinch-Old course	True Links	2007
Lahinch-Lahinch-Castle course	True Links	2012
Doonbeg-Doonbeg Golf Club	True Links	2006
Milltown On Malbay-Spanish Point (9 Holes)	Links	2007
County Galway		
Ballyconneely-Connemara-Championship course	True Links	2007
Ballyconneely-Connemara-New course (9 Holes)	True Links	2007
Renvyle-Renvyle House Hotel (9 Holes)	Seaside	2007
Annaghuane-Connemara Isles Golf Club (9 Holes)	Links	2007
County Mayo		
Bellmullet-Carne Golf Club	True Links	2003
Keel-Achill Island Golf Club (9 Holes)	True Links	2007
Mulranny-Mulranny Golf Club (9 Holes)	Links	2012

County Kerry		
Ballybunion-Ballybunion Golf Club-Old course	True Links	2009
Ballybunion-Ballybunion Golf Club-Cashen course	True Links	1990
Ballyferriter-Dingle Links (9 Holes)	Links	2006
Castlegregory-Castlegregory Golf Club	Links	2006
Glenbeigh-Dooks Golf Club	True Links	2011
Tralee-Tralee Golf Club	True Links	2009
Waterville-Waterville Golf Club	True Links	2011
County Dublin		
Dublin-Portmarnock Golf Club-Championship	True Links	2007
Dublin-Portmarnock Golf Club-Yellow (9 Holes)	True Links	2012
Dublin-Portmarnock Hotel and Golf Links	True Links	2009
Dublin-Rush Golf Club (9 Holes)	Links	2012
Dublin-St. Annes Golf Club	Links	2009
Dublin-Royal Dublin	Links	1990
Dublin-Sutton Golf Club (9 Holes)	Links	2010
Donabate-Corballis	True Links	2012

Donabate-The Island Golf Club	True Links	2009
County Louth		
Drogheda-Seapoint	Links	2009
Drogheda-County Louth	True Links	2004
County Meath		
Bettystown-Laytown and Bettystown	Links	2009
County Cork		
Kinsale-Old Head Golf Club	Clifftop	2009
Castletownbere-Berehaven (9 Holes)	Seaside	2011
County Waterford		
Dungarvan-Gold Coast Golf and Leisure	Seaside	2009
County Wexford		
Rosslare-Rosslare Golf Club	True Links	2009
Rosslare-Rosslare Golf Club-Burrow (12 Holes)	True Links	2013
County Wicklow		
Brittas Bay-The European Club	True Links	2006

Wicklow-Wicklow Golf Club	Clifftop	2009
Arklow-Arklow Golf Club	Links	2009

Northern Ireland

County Antrim	Type of Course	Last Year Played
Ballycastle-Ballycastle Golf Club	Links/ Parkland	2007
Larne-Larne Golf Club (9 Holes)	Links/ Clifftop	2007
Portballintrae-Bushfoot Golf Club (9 Holes)	Links	2007
Portrush-Royal Portrush-Dunluce course	True Links	2014
Portrush-Royal Portrush-Valley course	True Links	2007
County Down		
Ardglass-Ardglass Golf Club	Clifftop	2011
Newcastle-Royal County Down-Championship course	True Links	2014
Newcastle-Royal County Down-Annesley course	True Links	2011
Cloughey-Kirkistown Castle Golf Club	True Links	2011
County Londonberry		

Castlerock-Castlerock Golf Club-Mussenden course	Links	2007
Castlerock-Castlerock Golf Club-Bann course (9 Holes)	True Links	2012
Portstewart-Portstewart Golf Club-Old course	Links/ Parkland	2012
Portstewart-Portstewart Golf Club-Strand course.	Links/ Seaside	2013
Portstewart-Portstewart Golf Club-Riverside course.	Links/ Seaside	2012

Scotland

Scottish Borders	Type of Course	Last Year Played
Eyemouth-Eyemouth Golf Club	Clifftop	2011
East Lothian		
Aberlady-Kilspindie Golf Club	Links	2008
Aberlady-Craigielaw	Links	2014
Dunbar-Dunbar Golf Club	True Links	2008
Dunbar-Winterfield Golf Club	Links	2014
Gullane-Gullane No. 1	True Links	2005
Gullane-Gullane No. 2	Links	1991

Gullane-Gullane No. 3	Links	2008
Gullane-Muirfield	Links	2008
Gullane-Luffness New	True Links	2008
Gullane-Rennaissance	Links	2014
Gullane-Archerfield Dirleton Links	Seaside	2005
Longniddry-Longniddry Golf Club	Links	2008
Musselburgh-Musselburgh Links (9 Holes)	True Links	2008
North Berwick-North Berwick West Links	True Links	2008
North Berwick-Glen	Clifftop	2008
Fife		
Anstruther-Anstruther Golf Club (9 Holes)	Links	2014
Crail-Crail Golfing Society-Balcomie Links	Links	2014
Elie-Golf House Club	True Links	2008
Leven-Leven Golf Club	True Links	2008
Lundin-Lundin Links	True Links	2008
St. Andrews-The Old Course	True Links	2005
St. Andrews-The New Course	True Links	1988

St. Andrews-Jubilee Course	True Links	2014
St. Andrews-Eden Course	True Links	2014
St. Andrews-Strathtyrum Course	True Links	2014
St. Andrews-Castle Course	Seaside	2014
St. Andrews-St. Andrews Bay Hotel-Torrance	Seaside	2014
St. Andrews-St. Andrews Bay Resort-Devlin	Seaside	2014
Kingsbarns-Kingsbarn Golf Club	Links/ Seaside	2005
Highlands		
Arsaig-Traigh Golf Club (9 Holes)	Links	2012
Brora-Brora Golf Club	True Links	2010
Culloden-Castle Stuart Golf Club	Links/ Seaside	2010
Dornoch-Royal Dornoch Golf Club	True Links	1989
Dornoch-Royal Dornoch Golf Club-Struie	True Links	2012
Durness-Durness Golf Club (9 Holes)	True Links	2010
Fortrose-Fortrose and Rosemarkie Golf Club	Links	2010
Gairloch-Gairloch Golf Club (9 Holes)	Seaside	2012
Golspie-Golspie Golf Club	Links	2010

Nairn-Nairn Golf Club	Links	2005
Nairn-Nairn Dunbar Golf Club	Links	2010
Reay-Reay Golf Club	Links	2010
Tain-Tain Golf Club	True Links	2010
Tarbat-Tarbat Golf Club (9 Holes)	Links	2012
Wick-Wick Golf Club	True Links	2010
Moray		
Buckie-Strathlene Golf Club	Clifftop	2010
Cullen-Cullen Golf Club	Seaside	2010
Hopeman-Hopeman Golf Club	Links	2012
Lossiemouth-Moray Golf Club-Old	True Links	2010
Lossiemouth-Moray Golf Club-New	True Links	2010
Spey Bay-Spey Bay Golf Club	True Links	2010
Angus		
Barry-Panmure Golf Club	Links	2008
Arbroath-Arbroath Golf Club	Links	2010
Carnoustie-Carnoustie Golf Club-Championship	True Links	1989

Carnoustie-Carnoustie Golf Club-Burnside	Links	2014
Carnoustie-Carnoustie Golf Club-Buddon Links	Links	2014
Monifieth-Monifieth Golf Club-Medal	Links	2010
Monifieth-Monifieth Golf Club-Ashludie	Links/Seaside	2014
Montrose-Montrose Golf Club-Medal	True Links	2010
Montrose-Montrose Golf Club-Broomfield	True Links	2010

Aberdeenshire

Cruden Bay-Cruden Bay	True Links	2008
Cruden Bay-St. Olaf (9 Holes)	True Links	2014
Fraserburgh-Fraserburgh Golf Club-Corbie	True Links	2010
Fraserburgh-Fraserburgh Golf Club-Rosehill	Links	2014
Inverallochy-Inverallochy Golf Club	Links/ Clifftop	2010
Macduff-Royal Tarlair Golf Club	Links/ Clifftop	2010
Newburgh-Newburgh on Ythan Golf Club	Links	2010
Peterhead-Peterhead Golf Club	Links/ Seaside	2005
Balmedie-Trump International Golf Links	True Links	2014

Aberdeen City

Aberdeen-Balnagask Golf Club	Links/ Seaside	2014
Aberdeen-Kings Links	True Links	2014
Aberdeen-Royal Aberdeen Club	True Links	1995
Aberdeen-Murcar Golf Club	True Links	2008
Warkworth-Warkworth Golf Club (9 Holes)	Links	2014
Dumfries and Galloway		
Cummertrees-Powfoot Golf Club	Links/ Parkland	2007
Glenluce-Wigtownshire Golf Club	Links	2007
Monreith-St. Medan Golf Club (9 Holes)	Seaside	2007
Portpatrick-Portpatrick Golf Club	Seaside	2007
Southerness-Southerness Golf Club	True Links	2007
South Ayrshire		
Barassie-Kilmarnock Golf Club (27 Holes)	Links	2007
Prestwick-Prestwick Golf Club	True Links	2007
Prestwick-Prestwick St. Nicholas Golf Club	True Links	2007
Troon-Royal Troon Golf Club-Old Course	True Links	2007
Troon-Royal Troon Golf Club-Portland Course	Links	2007

Troon-Troon Municipal-Lochgreen Course	Links	2007
Troon-Troon Municipal-Darley Course	Links	2007
Troon-Troon Municipal-Fullarton Course	Seaside	2007
Turnberry-Ailsa	True Links	2007
Turnberry-Kintyre	Links/Park-land	2007
North Ayrshire		
Irvine-Glasgow Gailes	Links	2007
Irvine-Western Gailes	True Links	2007
Irvine-Dundonald Golf Club	True Links	2007
Irvine-Irvine Golf Club	Links	2007
West Kilbride-West Kilbride Golf Club	Links	2007
Isles		
Sconser-Isle of Skye Golf Club (9 Holes)	True Links	2012
Isle of Harris-Scarista (9 Holes)	True Links	2007
Isle of Arran-Shiskine Golf Club (12 Holes)	True Links	2007
Isle of Arran-Machrie Bay Golf Club (9 Holes)	Links	2007
Isle of Islay-Machrie Hotel Golf Club	True Links	1998

South Uist-Askernish Golf Club	True Links	2012
Barra-Barra Golf Club (9 Holes)	True Links	2012
Isle of Colonsay-Isle of Colonsay Golf Club (9 Holes)	True Links	2012
Isle of Mull-Tobermory Golf Club (9 Holes)	Clifftop	2014
Isle of Mull-Craignure Golf Club (9 Holes)	Seaside	2014
Isle of Bute-Kingarth-Bute Golf Club (9 Holes)	Links	2014
Isle of Tiree (9 Holes)	True Links	2014
Argyll		
Machrihanish-Machrihanish Golf Club	True Links	2010
Machrihanish-Machrihanish Dunes Golf Club	True Links	2010
Carradale-Carradale Golf Club (9 Holes)	Clifftop	2012
Dunaverty-Dunaverty Golf Club	Links	2012
North Ayrshire		
Irvine-Glasgow Gailes	Links	2007
Irvine-Western Gailes	True Links	2007

Wales

Isle of Anglesey	Type of Course	Last Year Played
Amlwch-Bull Bay Golf Club	Links/Clifftop	2006
Holyhead-Holyhead Golf Club	Seaside	2006
Rhosneigr-Anglesey Golf Club	Links	2006
Bridgend		
Bridgend-Southerdown Golf Club	Links/Clifftop	2006
Porthcawl-Porthcawl Golf Club	True Links	2006
Plye-Pyle and Kenfig Golf Club	Links	2013
Carthmarthenshire		
Burry Point-Ashburnham Golf Club	Links	2006
Ceredigion		
Borth-Borth and Ynyslas Golf Club	True Links	2006
Cardigan-Cardigan Golf Club	Clifftop	2006
Conwy		

Conwy-Conwy Golf Club	True Links	2006
Llandudno-Llandudno(Maesdu) Golf Club	Links/ Parkland	2006
Llandudno-North Wales Golf Club	True Links	2006
Denbighshire		
Prestatyn-Prestatyn Golf Club	Links	2006
Rhyl-Rhyl Golf Club (9 Holes) .	Links	2006
Gwynedd		
Abersoch-Abersoch Golf Club	Links	2006
Aberdovey-Aberdovey Golf Club	True Links	2006
Harlech-Royal St. Davids	True Links	2006
Morfa Nefyn-Nefyn and District	Clifftop	2006
Porthmadog-Porthmadog Golf Club	Links/ Seaside	2006
Pwllheli-Pwllheli Golf Club	Links/ Parkland	2006
Pembrokeshire		
St. David's-St. David's City (9 Holes)	Links	2013
Tenby-Tenby Golf Club	True Links	2006
Newport Golf Links	Links/ Seaside	2013

Swansea		
Southgate-Pennard Golf Club	True Links	2006
Glamorgan-Swansea Bay	Links	2006

Acknowledgments
And Heartfelt Gratitude

~~~

Jo and I are forever grateful to so many who helped us through this heartbreak in the days and months that followed the accident. While I would love to name everyone, I must acknowledge the unconditional friendship of Greg and Jennifer Currie, Ronny and Susan Brown, Randy and Dianne Dorton, John and Guyann Fraley, and John Lineberger. They stayed constantly by our side for over a week and held us up. Each deserves stars in their crown on the final Day of Judgment. We are totally in your debt.

Words are wholly inadequate to express the gratitude we also feel to so many who helped us honor Sally's beautiful legacy by fulfilling our vision of building Sally's Y. Again, I would love to acknowledge everyone and could fill this entire book with your names. However, without my two brothers Allison and Walter, my sister Caroline, Steve and Karen Cummings and their family, and Greg and India Keith and their family's personal and financial support, and their own love for Sally, we couldn't have done it. Beyond this help, without the never ending support and help of Andy Calhoun, Lynn Lomax, Mary Tucker, Dean Jones, and Ron Johnston who work for the Y, we would also not have been able to achieve our vision. Mary Tucker dedicated her life to our quest and deserves stars in her crown for what she did for us.

It also goes beyond words to say how grateful we are to the Huntersville Police Department for their caring approach to our heartbreak. They showed sensitivity and compassion from the moment we arrived on the scene of the most devastating loss imaginable.

It would also be difficult not to express my heartfelt gratitude to the other woman in my life, Wanda Baker. She has helped me for more than 30 years, and without her help and guidance I would not have gotten very far in life.

This book would not have come to pass without the caring and thoughtful guidance of Ron Green, Jr. I am forever grateful.

While I cannot forgive him, as every day my heart aches for Sally, I hope David Scott Shimp finds a way to move forward in life. He will carry the heaviest burden imaginable, but, unlike the bar that served him, he took responsibility for his actions by pleading guilty to the charges he faced. I hope God helps him find his peace with that night that forever changed us all.

Made in the USA
San Bernardino, CA
11 December 2015